AMERICAN HISTORY FOR KIDS

Exploration, Battles, Tragedies, and Triumphs—
from Native Nations to the USA

STACIA DEUTSCH

Illustrated by Iratxe López de Munain

For general information on our other products and services or to obtain technical support, please contact our Customer Care Department within the United States at (866) 744-2665, or outside the United States at (510) 253-0500.

Rockridge Press publishes its books in a variety of electronic and print formats. Some content that appears in print may not be available in electronic books, and vice versa.

Series Designer: Tricia Jang
Interior and Cover Designer: Francesca Pacchini
Art Producer: Sue Bischofberger
Editor: Laura Apperson
Production Editor: Nora Milman
Production Manager: Martin Worthington

Illustration: © 2021 Iratxe López de Munain
Author Photo Courtesy of Val Westover Photography

Paperback ISBN: 978-1-64876-435-6
eBook ISBN: 978-1-64876-436-3
R0

CONTENTS

INTRODUCTION

When George Washington was elected to lead the United States of America, no one knew what to call him. He'd been called "General" during the Revolutionary War, but there was no title for the nation's first leader. Some suggested "Your Excellency." Others liked "His Highness." But the new constitution forbade titles of nobility. "Mr. President" was finally chosen, and it is still used today.

History tells us a lot about President Washington and his life. But American history began long before the first presidency, and so much has happened since. In this book, you'll get a new perspective on things you already know and read a lot of cool stuff you don't know yet.

Did you know that Abraham Lincoln was an excellent wrestler and was honored by Oklahoma's Wrestling Hall of Fame in 1992? Did you know the first documented discovery of a *T. rex* skeleton was in Montana in 1902? Did you know that in 1921, Bessie Coleman was the first Black woman and first Indigenous American woman to get a pilot's license?

American history is full of amazing people and interesting stories. Let's see what else we can discover.

CHAPTER 1

EARLIEST INHABITANTS

[20,000 BCE to 1400 CE]

How did early inhabitants arrive in the territory that would someday become the United States? One theory is that Indigenous Americans crossed a land bridge that existed during the Ice Age. About 11,000 years ago, the bridge was flooded, leaving several thousand stranded on the continent. Other scientists theorize that people traveled by sea in boats or canoes about 19,000 years ago. No matter how or when they arrived, these first Americans explored and settled their new home.

- **Tools made of stone and ivory from about 12,000 years ago were discovered in south central Montana.**
- **Clovis points are spear tips that trace back 13,500 years and have been found in more than 1,500 different archaeological sites.**
- **Mesoamericans are Indigenous American ancestors who lived in the area from central Mexico to Central America.**

EARLY INDIGENOUS AMERICANS

PEOPLE TO KNOW Between 100 CE and 1600 CE, the Anasazi lived mainly in what is now known as the Four Corners region where Utah, Colorado, New Mexico, and Arizona meet. Many built cliff homes high in the mountains.

STAT FACT **Between 800 CE and 1400 CE, the Hohokam of Arizona was the first early culture to use sophisticated canals to bring water to crops. By 1300 CE, the canal system was more than 700 miles (1,126 kilometers) long.**

- The Adena mainly lived in the Midwest from about 500 BCE to 100 CE and built mounds for burials. The mounds were mostly made of topsoil and clay, and some, like the Serpent Mound, were in the shapes of animals.

★ **Two thousand years ago, the Hopewell culture in the Ohio River Valley built large, broad geometric earthwork mounds in shapes like squares, circles, and octagons.**

PEOPLE TO KNOW The Mississippian culture spread throughout the Southeast around 1,000 years ago. Thousands of graves from that time have been found near Nashville, Tennessee. Around 1450 CE, the Mississippian people disappeared from the area, but no one knows where they went.

Tribes in the Mississippi River valley were farmers. They grew what are now called the "three sisters": corn, beans, and squash.

Mississippian copper plates

REGIONAL NATIONS OF NORTH AMERICA

PEOPLE TO KNOW For thousands of years, The Ojibwa were a migratory people. When they settled, they created communities primarily in what is now southern Canada and the midwestern United States.

Northwest cultures, like the Chinook, are known for carved totem poles.

- The **Yup'ik** of southwest Alaska share stories of their ancestors who sailed canoes called umiaks and harpooned whales.

TERM TO KNOW Pueblo architecture in the Southwest is made of limestone and dried mud bricks called **ADOBE**. The buildings could be five stories high, and people used ladders to get from floor to floor.

- The Nez Percé (also called the Nimi'ipuu), who lived on the Columbia Plateau in the Pacific Northwest, have been known for their Appaloosa horses, which have pale bodies with dark spots.

★ **Cultures in the Great Basin lived predominantly in what is now modern Utah and Montana. Anthropologists often separate these groups by whether they used horses or not.**

TERM TO KNOW Tribal communities throughout North America have many different and complex spiritual beliefs. One thing many have in common is the belief that all objects have a spirit or soul inside them. This is called **ANIMISM**.

IROQUOIS LEAGUE

- In the late 16th century, five Indigenous American Nations banded together to defend themselves against their enemies. The Five Nations, or Iroquois League, included the Mohawk, Oneida, Onondaga, Cayuga, and Seneca. They battled the Huron confederacy of the Bear, Cord, Rock, and Deer tribes.

PEOPLE TO KNOW **HIAWATHA**, a Mohawk leader, and the **GREAT PEACEMAKER**, also known as Dekanawida, convinced tribes that had traditionally battled to join together to establish peace.

In 1722, the Tuscarora became the sixth nation to join the Iroquois League. The league is now known as the Six Nations.

Mohawk

★ Though American poet Henry Wadsworth Longfellow's poem "The Song of Hiawatha" is about an Ojibwa warrior and is not connected to the Iroquois League, it still made the name "Hiawatha" popular.

TERM TO KNOW **WAMPUM BELTS** are beaded artworks that record important events. Each symbol on the Hiawatha belt represents one of the original Nations in the Iroquois League.

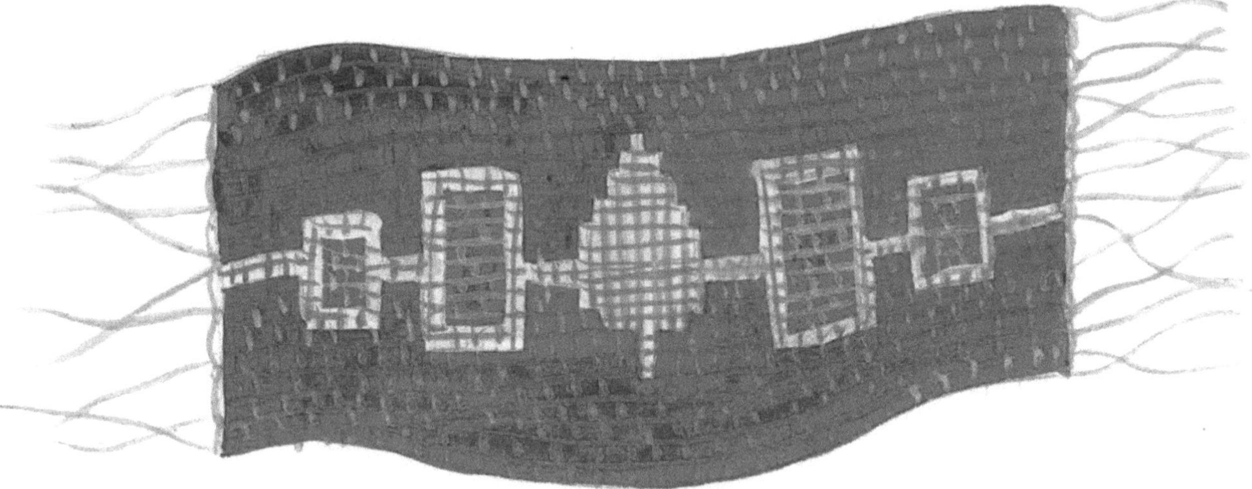

➧ Each Nation in the Iroquois League had representation in their confederacy and came together to decide important issues. Early American politicians were influenced by this model of a representative democracy.

CHAPTER 2

THE AGE OF EXPLORATION

[1400 CE to 1800 CE]

The Age of Exploration is a period when the richest and most powerful European nations searched the world to increase trade and expand their empires. Thanks to new technologies like the astrolabe and compass, sailors were able to chart their location and direction while sailing and share more accurate maps. As people traded goods, money flowed into Europe. However, violence, disease, and slavery were also results of exploration. Exploration connected people and places that had never been connected before, forever changing the world.

- **Increased trade with Asia let Europeans learn more about geography and navigation.**
- **Spain and Portugal competed to see who could sail the farthest, the fastest and claim the most territories.**
- **European empires gained wealth by forming colonies in the Americas. They looked for gold, silver, and other things to trade.**

PIRATES

STAT FACT **There were so many pirates between 1650 and 1730 it was called the Golden Age of Piracy. During that time, as many as 5,000 pirates are thought to have been at sea.**

PEOPLE TO KNOW Around 1717, British sailor Edward Teach became the notorious pirate **BLACKBEARD**. He was known to attack settlements in the Caribbean Sea and along the Atlantic Coast, stealing anything valuable.

- Many pirates came from poverty and needed a way to make money. Piracy was a rough life but offered more opportunities than staying in crowded towns with few jobs.

EXPLORING THE GLOBE

PEOPLE TO KNOW **PRINCE HENRY THE NAVIGATOR** of Portugal was the first person known to encourage global exploration. He sponsored the trade of enslaved people and gold from West Africa.

- Explorers discovered they could get wealthy by selling sugar. They searched for new places to produce sugar with cheap labor, like Brazil and the West Indies, which led to slavery.

★ **When Europeans first brought pigs to the Americas, they multiplied quickly and destroyed crops. In New York, the place where a wall was built to keep pigs away is now called Wall Street.**

TERM TO KNOW **THE MIDDLE PASSAGE** was one leg of a triangular trade route where enslavers traded goods like iron, cloth, and guns for African enslaved people. The enslavers then traded those enslaved people to other countries for items like sugar and tobacco.

STAT FACT **Between the years 1526 and 1867, more than 12 MILLION African people were enslaved and brought to the Americas where enslavers forced them to work.**

- In Missouri, there were laws against teaching enslaved people to read and write. Anyone who did so would be fined and could go to jail. Some brave Missourians, like John Berry Meachum, started secret schools.

PORTUGUESE EXPEDITIONS

- Portuguese sailors searched for a sea route to Asia by sailing south around Africa. On their travels they mapped the coasts of Africa, Asia, and Brazil.

PEOPLE TO KNOW **VASCO DA GAMA** was the first Portuguese sailor to reach India in 1498. He had four ships on his mission. The voyage marked a new time of discovery and trade.

Vasco da Gama

★ **Cape of Good Hope is a rocky cove on the Atlantic coast of South Africa. Originally called Cape of Storms, it was renamed to encourage people to use the route to India and the East.**

★ **Prince Henry the Navigator wasn't a sailor or a navigator, and he wasn't called by that name until more than 300 years after his death. He was born Dom Henrique of Portugal, Duke of Viseu, the fourth child of Portuguese King John I.**

In 1519, Portuguese explorer Ferdinand Magellan organized the first complete voyage around the globe.

★ **Ferdinand Magellan's crew ran out of food while sailing across the Pacific Ocean. They ate rats, sawdust, and rope to survive. Even then, only 18 of the original 265 men made it home.**

Trade Routes

SPANISH EXPLORATION

Conquistadors led the Spanish conquest of the Americas.

In the late 15th century, Spain funded an expedition led by Italian explorer Christopher Columbus. The Spanish hoped to get around Portugal's established routes and make their own, but Columbus was unsuccessful.

TERM TO KNOW **CONQUISTADORS** were the soldier-explorers that came after Columbus. They led the Spanish conquest of the Americas. These armed soldiers were able to move fast on horseback. They strove to conquer Indigenous people, find riches, and convert the tribes to Christianity.

Instead of finding a western trade route to Asia, Columbus landed in the Americas.

★ Columbus set sail on August 3, 1492. On the difficult trip, his men threatened mutiny. Columbus promised them that if they didn't find land, he would turn the boats around, but he didn't mean it.

Columbus' ship, the *Santa Maria*

★ Columbus had four voyages. On his last one, he survived a hurricane, an attack by Indigenous tribes, and a mutiny by his men. Columbus had to be rescued by Spain from Jamaica.

PEOPLE TO KNOW In 1521, **HERNÁN CORTÉS** conquered the Aztecs and claimed Mexico for Spain. He destroyed the capital city, Tenochtitlán, and captured Emperor Cuauhtémoc. The battle lasted three months.

ENGLISH EXPEDITIONS

- Many English expeditions were planned in order to convert Indigenous people to Christianity. The explorers and sailors, however, were more interested in trade and riches.

British Commonwealth Symbol

PEOPLE TO KNOW In 1497, Italian explorer **JOHN CABOT** claimed the land he discovered for the British king. He thought it was Asia, but he'd actually discovered a short route to North America.

- At its height, the British Empire was the largest in history. From early exploration onward, the British brought colonies and territories under their rule. Today, most countries that were once in the British Commonwealth are independent.

PEOPLE TO KNOW **SIR WALTER RALEIGH** was an English explorer and poet. After his second mission to America, he got married without the Queen's permission and spent 12 years in jail in the Tower of London.

STAT FACT **The Jamestown settlement in Virginia was the first permanent British colony. In 1607, 104 men and boys arrived to start the settlement. By 1610, 80 to 90 PERCENT had died from starvation and disease.**

There is no evidence that Plymouth Rock is where the Pilgrims took their first steps into America in 1620.

FRENCH EXPEDITIONS

- Spanish influence in North America decreased as the French, Dutch, and British took over trade routes, sped up exploration, and set up their own protected colonies in the late 1500s.

PEOPLE TO KNOW In 1534, navigator **JACQUES CARTIER** claimed the area around the St. Lawrence River as New France. Though he never sent valuables home or established a colony himself, New France lasted more than 200 years.

The French created trading outposts throughout New France. Local hunters traded beaver pelts for French goods, supplies, and glass beads.

PEOPLE TO KNOW **SAMUEL DE CHAMPLAIN** explored the Caribbean in 1601. He also explored northern New York and the Great Lakes. In 1608, he founded what would become Quebec City, one of Canada's oldest cities.

- Champlain made an alliance with the Indigenous American Huron and Algonquian people. Champlain also agreed to help them fight against the Iroquois, now known as Haudenosaunee.

★ **The French word "ville" means city. Many cities in North America have -ville at the end of their names because of French influence.**

EXPLORERS AND DISEASE

- The explorer Amerigo Vespucci described the Americas as "Mundus Novus," which means New World in Latin. Although the land was new to Europeans, people had lived in the Americas for thousands of years.

★ **When Europeans traveled back and forth across the Atlantic, they brought plants, animals, and diseases with them.**

Indigenous Peoples had never been exposed to chickenpox, measles, mumps, and smallpox, and many were unable to survive these diseases.

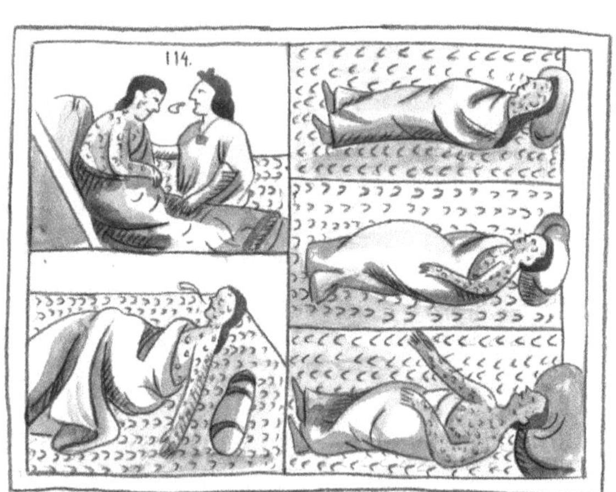

TERM TO KNOW In 1972, historian Alfred W. Crosby coined the term **COLUMBIAN EXCHANGE** to define the period when Europeans first brought diseases, plants, and animals to the Americas.

STAT FACT **A hundred years after Christopher Columbus's arrival in the Americas, nearly 55 MILLION people had died from the disease and violence brought by settlers.**

- Doctors and surgeons were important on explorer ships. They took care of sickness, wrapped broken bones, and patched the wounded in raids and battles. Columbus took medical staff on his voyages.

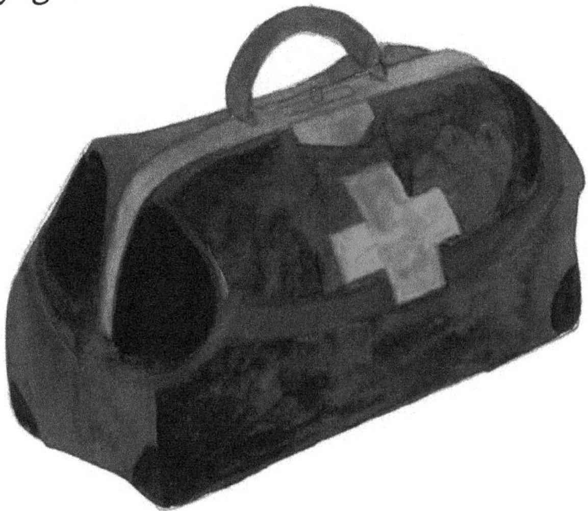

EXPLORERS AND AGRICULTURE

★ Europeans introduced cows and pigs to the Americas. On their voyages back to Europe, they took llamas and turkeys, two animals that had never been there before.

➧ New foods often required workers who knew how to farm them. Rice was popular in the new colonies, so explorers enslaved people from Africa who knew how to grow it.

★ The potato had never grown in Europe before explorers brought it with them from the Americas. In a short time, potatoes became very important, especially in Ireland where they became a nutritious addition to most diets.

Explorers brought horses, cattle, and sheep to the Americas. Depending on what they needed, Indigenous people used these easily domesticated animals for hunting, logging, hauling, food, and travel.

Columbus brought sugarcane on his second voyage. It became so valuable that some British colonists called sugar "white gold."

★ **Many animals were brought to the Americas on purpose, but some came by accident. Brown rats, zebra mussels, and earthworms snuck in on the ships.**

Explorers accidentally brought zebra mussels to the Americas.

PLACES NAMED FOR NEW WORLD EXPLORERS

PEOPLE TO KNOW **AMERIGO VESPUCCI** was a Florentine explorer who went on voyages to the Americas. In the 1500s, mapmakers used the word "America," an adaptation of the name Amerigo, to label the area.

STAT FACT **FIFTY-FOUR** cities in the United States of America are named for Christopher Columbus, including Columbia, Missouri; Columbus, Georgia; and Columbus, Kentucky.

★ A crater on Mars and a lab on the International Space Station are both named after Christopher Columbus.

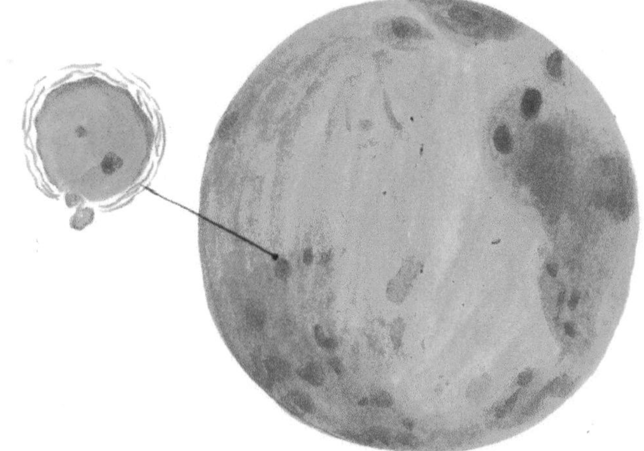

- The state of Louisiana was named in honor of King Louis XIV by the French explorer René-Robert Cavelier, Sieur de La Salle. He claimed the area of the Mississippi River and its tributaries for France.

PEOPLE TO KNOW Strong ocean winds forced **HENRY HUDSON**, a Dutch explorer, to sail down a river in New York and New Jersey in 1609. The Hudson River is now named for him.

Hudson's *Half Moon* ship

- The town Captain Cook on the island of Hawaii is named for the English explorer who was likely the first European to visit.

EARLY EUROPEAN SETTLEMENTS

TERM TO KNOW **COLONIZATION** is the process of settling in a new territory. It also means taking over someone else's land to use for yourself by force.

- As settlements began, colonizers grew crops to gain wealth. The increased demand for tobacco and sugar required more field workers. After 1600, the colonizers enslaved many more people from Africa and brought them to North America.

- Europeans had set up villages in Ireland and thought they could do the same in America, but the land was very different. The heat, bugs, and lack of experience caused many deaths.

STAT FACT During exploration and settlement, up to **5.5 MILLION** Indigenous Americans were forced into slavery in the Americas. Another **12.5 MILLION** enslaved people were from Africa.

★ Roanoke Island in North Carolina is called the Lost Colony because an attempt to build a settlement there failed. Around 1590, there was a search for the settlers, but they were gone. Their fate remains unknown.

★ Fort Caroline was an attempted French settlement in Florida. In 1565, Spanish settlers destroyed the French fort and built their own. In 1568, the French attacked the Spanish and destroyed it again.

CHAPTER 3

THE THIRTEEN COLONIES

[1606–1776]

The original 13 British colonies were founded between 1606 and 1732. These were New Hampshire, Massachusetts, Connecticut, Rhode Island, New York, New Jersey, Pennsylvania, Delaware, Maryland, Virginia, North Carolina, South Carolina, and Georgia. In 1776, they would become the United States of America. Since the colonies were under British rule, any money earned in America was heavily taxed for England. But for many settlers, colonial life provided religious freedoms and new opportunities.

- **Virginia Dare is known to be the first English child born in the original 13 colonies in 1587.**
- **Because England wasn't as rich or powerful as Spain, it didn't settle colonies in America until nearly 100 years after Columbus arrived.**
- **Georgia was named for King George II and Virginia was named after Queen Elizabeth, who was known as the Virgin Queen.**

JAMESTOWN AND PLYMOUTH

STAT FACT **THREE** ships carrying **104** men arrived in 1607 to settle in Jamestown, Virginia. It was the first permanent English settlement.

- Powhatan was the Pamunkey leader of the Indigenous Nations around Jamestown. In 1613, the British kidnapped Powhatan's daughter, Pocahontas, and forced her to marry a settler, John Rolfe.

PEOPLE TO KNOW **WILLIAM BRADFORD** was the governor of Plymouth Colony for 30 years. His book *Of Plymouth Plantation*, written from 1630 to 1651, describes how the settlers struggled to survive in the colony.

NEW ENGLAND COLONIES

- The early Puritan settlers in Plymouth, Massachusetts, were people who came to practice their religion freely. But conflicts with non-Puritans led some to leave the colony and start their own villages in Rhode Island, Connecticut, and New Hampshire.

PEOPLE TO KNOW **ANNE HUTCHINSON** refused to follow Puritan Christian traditions. She was kicked out of the Massachusetts Bay Colony and moved to Rhode Island, establishing a settlement there.

TERM TO KNOW The **TRIANGULAR TRADE** was a cycle where New England shippers would sell rum in exchange for enslaved African people. Then they'd sell the enslaved people to the West Indies for molasses to make more rum.

- The New England colonies were famous for marine businesses like whaling, shipbuilding, and fishing. These businesses led to other associated crafts, like making sails and ropes and producing lumber to build boats.

★ **Wealthy colonial landowners often wore large powdered wigs to keep up with the popular fashion in England. The wigs were powdered with starch and lavender because they smelled terrible and attracted bugs.**

The Hartford Courant, established as the *Connecticut Courant*, is the oldest continuously published newspaper in the United States. It was established in 1764 in Hartford, Connecticut.

Large powdered wigs were fashionable in colonial New England.

SOUTHERN COLONIES

TERM TO KNOW **PLANTATIONS** were large farms where enslaved people were forced to work. Settlers built houses and had the fields planted with crops to establish permanent homes in the colonies. Many plantations in the southern colonies grew tobacco, sugarcane, rice, cotton, and indigo, which was a purple dye.

Georgia was the last of the 13 colonies to be established.

- Warm weather brought diseases like yellow fever and malaria. Though many people lived to old age, the average life span for a Southern colonist was 35 years.

Sugarcane was commonly grown on Southern plantations.

MIDDLE COLONIES

➧ The middle colonies attracted settlers because they were open to diverse religious beliefs. Many of these new immigrants were not wealthy but could afford their own passage from Europe.

Old Swedes Church, Philadelphia, PA

PEOPLE TO KNOW **WILLIAM PENN** founded the Province of Pennsylvania in 1681. Despite his work and the growth of settlements in the area, he was thrown into prison in England. He died penniless.

★ **The middle colonies were called the "breadbasket" because they provided so much food to the other two regions. There was good, healthy soil, and the colonists grew many crops, including wheat.**

FRENCH AND INDIAN WAR AND THE PROCLAMATION OF 1763

The French and Indian War was a North American conflict between France and Great Britain from 1754 to 1763. During the war, Indigenous allies fought with the French colonists, while the Iroquois Confederacy joined the British in battle.

Twenty-two-year-old George Washington led British soldiers as a lieutenant colonel in the French and Indian War.

The lyrics for the song "Yankee Doodle" are thought to have been made up by the British in the French and Indian War to tease the colonists. During the Revolutionary War, American soldiers adapted the words.

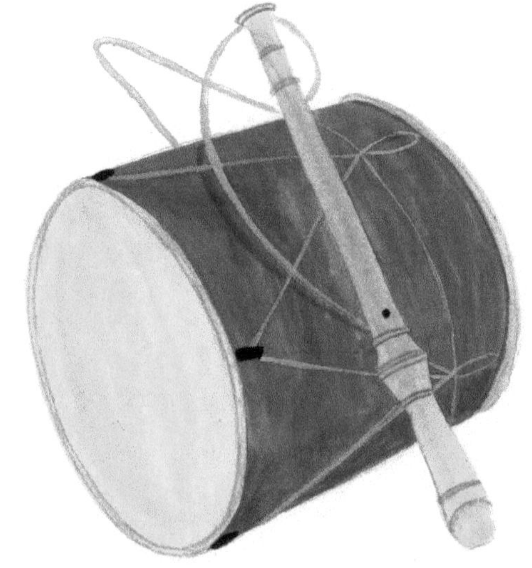

- The British Proclamation of 1763 was issued after the British won the French and Indian War. It declared that colonists were forbidden to settle on the Indigenous American land west of the Appalachian Mountains.

★ **Some settlers ignored the British Proclamation of 1763 because the best farmland was on the other side of the Appalachians, so they moved there anyway.**

- King George III issued the Proclamation of 1763 because he wanted to control the territory and thought that new taxes would pay for the war. Instead, the proclamation just made the colonists mad.

SUGAR ACT AND STAMP ACT

- Colonists smuggled sugar and molasses from the French and Dutch West Indies because they didn't have to pay taxes on these non-British goods. The British wanted the colonists to buy from Britain only, so they introduced the Sugar Act of 1764 that effectively made their sugar cheaper.

TERM TO KNOW **DEBT** is borrowed money that needs to be paid back. The money raised from the Sugar Act would help Britain pay their debt from the French and Indian War.

- The Sugar Act also limited trade and commerce by requiring that businesses in the colonies could only sell certain things, like iron and lumber, to England and nowhere else.

- Still needing money to pay debts, England signed the Stamp Act in 1765. All paper documents, including playing cards and newspapers, needed to have an official stamp on them that showed that the British tax had been paid.

Official British tax stamp

PEOPLE TO KNOW **PATRICK HENRY** was a colonist opposed to British control and the Stamp Act. In a famous speech, he declared, "Give me liberty or give me death!"

★ **In Boston, resisters to the Stamp Act called themselves the Sons of Liberty. They forced Andrew Oliver, the stamp distributor, to resign. By 1766, most distributors had left their jobs.**

TOWNSHEND ACTS AND INTOLERABLE ACTS

- In 1767, the British created more taxes for the colonies with the Townshend Acts. They taxed paint, lead, paper, and tea.

★ **"No taxation without representation" is a slogan that originated in the colonies. It meant that the people didn't want to pay taxes to England without having a voice in how the colonies were ruled.**

- On March 5, 1770, British soldiers shot into a crowd of people protesting taxes. Five men died in the event that would be called the Boston Massacre. In April, Britain repealed all the Townshend taxes except the one on tea.

TERM TO KNOW In 1774, England passed five laws against the colonies that became known as the Intolerable Acts. **INTOLERABLE** is when something cannot be accepted because it is too harsh. People refused to accept the laws because they unfairly took power away from the colonists.

STAT FACT **During the Boston Tea Party on December 16, 1773, colonists angry about the Townshend Acts dumped 342 chests of British tea into Boston Harbor. Four of the Intolerable Acts were direct punishments for the Boston Tea Party.**

The Intolerable Acts united the colonies and brought them closer to a war for independence.

JOHN LOCKE

PEOPLE TO KNOW **JOHN LOCKE** was born on August 29, 1632, in England. Though he never went to the colonies, his book *The Second Treatise of Government* influenced future US president Thomas Jefferson, who also believed a ruler must represent people.

- Locke believed in religious tolerance and the importance of education. He wrote that people should have a say in how they are governed, and if not, have the right to overthrow the ruler.

★ **John Locke is less known for being a physician. He trained in medicine before he became involved in politics.**

THOMAS PAINE

PEOPLE TO KNOW The English writer **THOMAS PAINE** was born in 1737 and moved to Philadelphia in 1774. His 50-page pamphlet *Common Sense* argued for revolt against England. In a few months it sold more than 500,000 copies.

One of Paine's earliest pieces of writing condemned the enslavement of African people. He wrote this anonymously.

★ **Thomas Paine died alone in 1809. In 1819, an admirer dug up his bones and took them to England for an honorable burial, but the bones were eventually lost.**

BENJAMIN FRANKLIN

PEOPLE TO KNOW BENJAMIN FRANKLIN was born in Boston in 1706. Although he didn't have much education, he taught himself to read. Franklin opened a printing business in Philadelphia and would go on to become a Founding Father of the United States.

★ **Franklin was also an inventor who is credited with creating bifocal eyeglasses. He also conducted experiments with electricity and invented the lightning rod.**

- In 1754, Franklin first proposed uniting the colonies. The idea was rejected, but in 1777 it became the basis for the Articles of Confederation, which was the first constitution of the United States.

PHILLIS WHEATLEY

PEOPLE TO KNOW **PHILLIS WHEATLEY** is one of the best-known poets in early American history. Thirty-nine of her poems were published in 1773. This collection was the first published book by a Black American.

- Wheatley was enslaved when she was seven years old. Forced to leave her family, she traveled from West Africa, likely present-day Senegal or Gambia. Enslavers sold her to Boston commercialist John Wheatley and his wife, Susanna.

- The Wheatleys taught Phillis to read and write. They helped her publish her poems, although they kept her enslaved. They freed her shortly after her book was published.

GEORGE WASHINGTON

The first time George Washington ran for public office in Virginia in 1755, he lost. He always kept a copy of the poll that showed how each person voted.

When George Washtington was 11, he stopped attending school and was taught to run his family's tobacco farm instead.

In 1775, Washington became commander in chief of the Continental Army that fought the British for America's independence. Washington was a good commander, but he was an even better spy. He used code names and invisible ink.

THOMAS JEFFERSON

- Thomas Jefferson drafted the Declaration of Independence in 1776. He became the third president of the United States in 1801 after winning a tiebreaker with Aaron Burr.

★ **Jefferson liked archaeology, was an architect, studied wine, and was obsessed with books. When the Library of Congress needed books, he sold them his 6,500-volume collection.**

- Although Jefferson famously wrote in the Declaration of Independence, "All men are created equal," he enslaved more than 600 people in his lifetime.

DECLARATION OF INDEPENDENCE

Independence Hall, Philadelphia, PA

➧ The Declaration of Independence was the formal statement that the 13 colonies wanted to be free from British rule.

PEOPLE TO KNOW **MARY KATHARINE GODDARD** was the only woman whose name can be found on the Declaration of Independence. She was the printer who created the first copy of the official document. She added her name to the bottom of the document along with the original signers.

STAT FACT **Of the 56 men who signed the Declaration of Independence, 14 came from the New England colonies, 21 represented the middle colonies, and 21 represented the southern colonies.**

PEOPLE TO KNOW American **LOYALISTS** opposed the Declaration of Independence. These were colonists who wanted to remain subjects of England. **PATRIOTS** were those who supported the revolution.

About 20 percent of the people in the colonies were American Loyalists.

Independence was declared on July 2, 1776. The Declaration was adopted on July 4, but most signers didn't sign until August 2, and some delegates signed after that day.

SOLDIERS IN THE REVOLUTIONARY WAR

- The Revolutionary War was the colonists' fight against the British for independence. The war lasted from 1775 to 1783, and many major battles happened after America declared independence in 1776.

- The Patriots, people who fought for American independence, were losing the war, so Benjamin Franklin went to France to ask for help. France joined the war on the side of the colonists in 1778.

★ **British troops were called Redcoats because of their red uniform. British soldiers were helped by some Indigenous Americans, paid German fighters, and loyal American colonists.**

TERM TO KNOW The American army during the Revolutionary War was called the **CONTINENTAL ARMY**. Anyone over the age of 16, or 15 with a parent's permission, could join.

- In April 1775, Lord Murray, Earl of Dunmore of Virginia, issued a proclamation offering freedom to anyone who escaped slavery and joined the British army. Soon thereafter, the Continental Army made the same promise.

★ **In Boston, a secret society at Harvard University began stealing the bodies of Revolutionary War casualties to study anatomy. Thieves called "resurrection men" would sell the bodies to Harvard and other local universities.**

WOMEN DURING THE REVOLUTION

PEOPLE TO KNOW **ABIGAIL ADAMS** was the wife of John Adams, the second president. She was a strong force in his life. When her husband was establishing the new government, she told him to "remember the ladies."

PEOPLE TO KNOW The **DAUGHTERS OF LIBERTY** was founded after the Stamp Act of 1765. The organization supported the revolution by sewing uniforms, making bullets, and fundraising for the war.

PEOPLE TO KNOW **MARY LUDWIG HAYS** is best known for delivering water to hot and tired soldiers to help sustain them. This earned her the name Molly Pitcher.

Mary Ludwig Hays, or Molly Pitcher

PEOPLE TO KNOW **DEBORAH SAMPSON** disguised herself as a man to join the Continental Army. She said her name was Robert Shurtleff. After more than a year of fighting, she was injured and her secret was discovered.

Deborah Sampson

PEOPLE TO KNOW **MERCY OTIS WARREN** wrote poems, plays, and opinion pieces about the war. Her plays often mocked British leaders. In 1805, she published a nonfiction historical account of the Revolutionary War.

PEOPLE TO KNOW **SYBIL LUDINGTON** is called the "female Paul Revere." At the age of 16, she rode 40 miles (64 kilometers) to warn Continental soldiers that the British had laid siege to Danbury, Connecticut.

LIFE AT WAR

★ **In New York, some British soldiers acted in plays. They did performances of six plays by William Shakespeare. They also wrote original plays that were pro-British and portrayed the soldiers as heroes.**

The British hired professional German troops called Hessians. More than 30,000 Hessian soldiers fought alongside the British during the war.

TERM TO KNOW The Continental Navy was the revolutionaries' naval fleet. It was made up of privately owned ships with sailors called **PRIVATEERS**. Their task was to disrupt British shipping and capture or destroy enemy ships.

- It was common for colonial children to finish schooling by age 10 after they learned to read and write, but some continued their education during the Revolutionary War.

PEOPLE TO KNOW **JOSEPH BRANT** was the English name of a Mohawk person named **THAYENDANEGEA**. He convinced many tribes to help the British fight against the colonists.

★ **The British wore the formal Redcoat uniforms, but the first colonial soldiers didn't have nice uniforms, and sometimes they had no uniforms at all. They wore brown because most people already owned a brown coat. Later, they wore blue.**

CHAPTER 4

UNITED STATES OF AMERICA

[1776-1800]

In 1776, the 13 colonies declared independence from England. The Revolutionary War ended in 1781 when the British surrendered at a battle in Yorktown, Virginia. The battle lasted 20 days and Colonel Alexander Hamilton led American forces to victory. Afterward, the British decided it wasn't worth continuing to fight the war. In 1782, Benjamin Franklin, John Adams, and John Jay negotiated peace in Paris with British representatives. It took many months, but on September 3, 1783, the Treaty of Paris was signed, and the British finally recognized the United States of America.

- **The Treaty of Paris stated that colonists who had supported the British would be treated fairly, even though they lost.**
- **Additional treaties were made to keep peace after the 1783 treaty.**
- **Only one agreement from the Treaty of Paris remains today: The original 13 colonies are still independent from England.**

ARTICLES OF THE CONSTITUTION

- The Constitution has a preamble and seven articles that lay out the way government works. It was signed in 1787 by delegates from the states.

- The first three articles of the Constitution describe the branches of government. The legislative branch, also known as Congress, makes laws. The executive branch is the office of the President. The judicial branch is the court system. The branches are meant to be equal in power.

STAT FACT The Constitution has **4,400** words. When it was signed there were **4 MILLION** people in the United States. In 2019, there were **329 MILLION**.

THE FIRST PRESIDENCY

- George Washington didn't want to be president at first. After leading the nation to victory on the battlefield, he wanted time off but the people asked him to run for president. On January 7, 1789, he was elected.

Washington and his wife lived in the Samuel Osgood house in New York City.

★ George Washington and his wife, Martha, never lived in the White House, because it hadn't been built yet. They lived in New York and Philadelphia.

★ In 1790, George Washington was invited to speak at the Touro Synagogue in Newport, Rhode Island. He declined the visit, but he wrote a letter committing to religious tolerance in America.

- The Electoral College is the representative body that casts the final vote for president. Washington is the only president to ever receive a unanimous Electoral College vote.

★ **George Washington's home, Mount Vernon, was near Alexandria, Virginia. His great grandfather bought the land in 1674. Mount Vernon is now on the National Register of Historic Places.**

PEOPLE TO KNOW **KATE** was an enslaved woman who worked at Washington's Mount Vernon, and she doesn't have a known last name. She was one of 317 enslaved people at the estate.

STAT FACT **Clocking in at TWO MINUTES, Washington's second inaugural address was the shortest ever given. It was a brief 135 words.**

In George Washington's farewell speech, he warned against political parties. He wanted citizens to see themselves as one American people.

- George Washington willingly stepped down after two terms, which became the custom for the presidency of the United States. After Franklin D. Roosevelt was elected to his fourth term in 1944, a two-term limit was added to the Constitution.

TERM TO KNOW Washington wanted to stay out of European politics. After King Louis XVI was beheaded in France in January 1793, the **NEUTRALITY PROCLAMATION** stated that America wouldn't take sides in the conflicts abroad.

- In 1789, George Washington proclaimed November 26 as the first national Thanksgiving Day. He celebrated in New York City by giving food and beer to city prisoners.

GOVERNMENT BEFORE WASHINGTON

The Continental Congress was the governing body of the colonies. From the end of the Revolution to Washington's election, the leader of the Congress was called president, but had no official power.

US Capitol Building

The Great Compromise of 1787 established a two-house system of government: the House of Representatives and the Senate.

TERM TO KNOW Population determined seats in the House of Representatives. A state's population was figured by counting free people, together with three-fifths of a state's enslaved people. This **THREE-FIFTHS COMPROMISE** gave the southern states more representation without any benefit to the enslaved themselves.

LEGISLATIVE BRANCH

➧ When the framers of the Constitution referred to Congress, they meant the House of Representatives and the Senate. They called this the "legislature" or "first branch" of the national government.

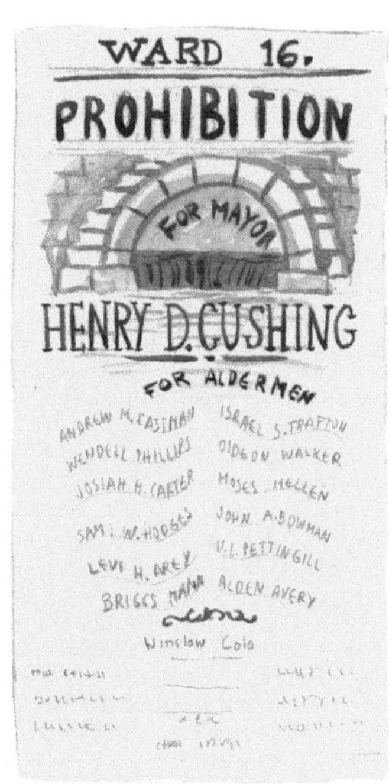

Early American Voting Ballot

★ **The American system of government is based on the British parliamentary system. When it was first established, senators were elected by government officials. Now they are elected by popular vote.**

TERM TO KNOW The founders established a system of **CHECKS AND BALANCES** so one branch would never have too much power. For example, the legislative branch can make a law, but the president can veto it.

JUDICIAL BRANCH

- The judicial branch is made up of courts and judges. Article III of the Constitution created the Supreme Court as the highest court in the land. The court's decisions take priority over all other courts.

- George Washington's Supreme Court had six justices who would serve until death or retirement. In 1869, President Ulysses S. Grant changed the number to nine, which has remained ever since. John Jay was the first Chief Justice.

★ **The first Supreme Court cases were in 1791.** *West v. Barnes* **was the first recorded decision, and the trial lasted just one day.**

EXECUTIVE BRANCH

- The president is the head of the executive branch and carries out laws made by the legislative branch. The president is also commander in chief of the armed forces and appoints the heads of federal agencies.

★ **In order to be president, a person must be at least 35, have lived in the United States for 14 years, and have been born a citizen of the United States.**

- An early version of the presidential seal was made in 1782. The eagle represents America and the 13 arrows represent the original states.

THE FIRST CABINET

PEOPLE TO KNOW The first cabinet of advisors, people who gave Washington advice, included Thomas Jefferson, Alexander Hamilton, Henry Knox, and Edmund Randolph. Washington sought opinions from others to gain different perspectives. Hamilton and Jefferson often disagreed.

- Alexander Hamilton was the first secretary of the treasury. He planned the First Bank of the United States, where the government's money is held, and the US Mint, where money is printed.

PEOPLE TO KNOW The first secretary of war was **HENRY KNOX**. He set up the national militia and evaluated their readiness. He was also in charge of the relationship with Indigenous Americans.

- The first secretary of state was Thomas Jefferson. His job was to negotiate with foreign countries and lead diplomatic meetings. Jefferson occasionally made decisions without telling the president.

- The first attorney general was Edmund Randolph. Washington wanted to make good legal decisions, so Randolph's job was to be the head of the Justice Department and chief law enforcement officer.

★ **In 1795, Edmund Randolph was accused of selling secret information to the French. The documents weren't valuable and he was innocent, but he resigned anyway.**

FEDERALISTS AND DEMOCRATIC-REPUBLICANS

- Thomas Jefferson and James Madison started a political party called the Democratic-Republicans. They advocated for states' rights through congressional representation.

TERM TO KNOW In a **REPUBLIC**, the power is held by the people through their representatives. The leader is a president who citizens vote for, rather than a king or a queen, who citizens cannot vote for.

TERM TO KNOW Alexander Hamilton believed in a single governing body and thought that America should have no states at all. This is the foundation of **FEDERALISM**.

Democratic-Republican political party ribbon

STAT FACT **Alexander Hamilton, John Jay, and James Madison wrote 85 essays explaining federalism, which were published as *The Federalist Papers*. Scholars believe Hamilton wrote 51 of the essays.**

★ **After serving as George Washington's vice president, John Adams was elected the second president of the United States. He was the first president to live in the White House.**

➧ In the election of 1800, Thomas Jefferson and Aaron Burr's joint ticket won, but it was tied for which one would be president and which vice president. The House of Representatives decided on Jefferson.

CHAPTER 5

WESTWARD EXPANSION

[1801–1861]

In 1775, there were nearly 2.5 million people living in the colonies. The colonists wanted more land to live and hunt on. President Jefferson negotiated a treaty with France in 1803 that gave the United States enough territory to double its size. People started exploring the newly acquired lands, which led to encounters with Indigenous Americans, new battles, and the desire to take even more land.

- **In 1775, pioneer and frontiersman Daniel Boone explored areas of Kentucky. He is best known for his wild tales about killing bears and fighting Indigenous people.**
- **Thomas Jefferson felt that owning land and working your own fields made people independent.**
- **In the mid-1800s the Pony Express was established to deliver mail. There were originally 80 deliverymen and between 400 and 500 horses.**

LOUISIANA PURCHASE

STAT FACT In 1803, Jefferson made a major deal with French emperor Napoleon called the Louisiana Purchase. For **$15 MILLION**, Jefferson purchased the land France had claimed west of the Mississippi River. It added **828,000** square miles (1.332 million square kilometers) and created **15** states.

★ Federalists in Congress opposed the Louisiana Purchase, since the Constitution wasn't clear if a president had power to purchase land. Even Jefferson was unclear, though he did it anyway.

➧ The Louisiana Purchase expanded slavery. As the new territory was divided into states, politics around slavery became heated and started the arguments that would eventually lead to the Civil War.

LEWIS AND CLARK

PEOPLE TO KNOW In 1804, Jefferson appointed **MERIWETHER LEWIS** to map and explore the lands west of the Mississippi. Lewis chose his own army commander, **WILLIAM CLARK**, and 45 others to join his Corps of Discovery, which started in Camp Wood, Illinois.

- The goal of Lewis and Clark's expedition was to find a **NORTHWEST PASSAGE**, a supposed water route that would connect the Atlantic and Pacific Oceans.

★ **Thomas Jefferson knew very little about what lay beyond the Rocky Mountains. He expected the expedition to find woolly mammoths and giant sloths.**

There were no woolly mammoths beyond the Rocky Mountains.

PEOPLE TO KNOW **YORK** was an enslaved man who William Clark brought on the mission. He hunted for food and cared for the sick along the way.

STAT FACT **While the explorers failed to find a Northwest Passage, they did reach the Pacific Ocean. They also collected 240 plant specimens and identified 122 new animals.**

★ **Two different birds were named for the explorers. Lewis's Woodpecker was discovered on July 20, 1805, and Clark's Nutcracker on August 22, 1805.**

Lewis's Woodpecker (left) and Clark's nutcracker (right).

SACAGAWEA

Statue of Sacajawea by Agnes Vincen Talbot, Sacajawea Center, Salmon, Idaho.

PEOPLE TO KNOW **SACAGAWEA** was a Shoshone person who was kidnapped by the Hidatsa Nation during a buffalo hunt in 1800. French-Canadian fur trader Toussaint Charbonneau either bought her or won her in a gambling game and made her his wife.

- In 1805, Sacagawea and her husband joined Lewis and Clark's journey. She spoke Shoshone and Hidatsa. Her husband spoke Hidatsa and French.

★ **The expedition met about 50 different Indigenous groups along the way and traded gifts like beads, knives, and tobacco. Sacagawea helped get horses from her brother, Chief Cameahwait.**

- When Sacagawea started traveling with Lewis and Clark, she was sixteen years old and six months pregnant. She gave birth to a boy named Jean-Baptiste Charbonneau, who William Clark nicknamed "Pompey."

★ **On January 6, 1806, there were reports of a beached whale near their camp by the Pacific Ocean. Sacagawea had never seen the ocean, so she joined the group of men who went to view the whale.**

- About three years after the journey, William Clark adopted Jean-Baptiste, promising to give him an education. After Sacagawea died in 1812, he adopted her daughter Lizette as well.

THE BEGINNING OF THE WAR OF 1812

- During the late 1700s, France and Britain were at war. The British decided to block the French from trading with America by capturing their ships.

TERM TO KNOW An **EMBARGO** is a ban on trade or commerce. The Embargo Act of 1807, signed by President Jefferson, closed American ports to all international trade until France and Britain ended their conflicts. This attempt to assert American rights failed, and the nation suffered economically.

- In 1808, James Madison became president. On June 8, 1812, he declared war against Britain over their trade restrictions and control of the seas.

★ **It took more than a month for the war declaration to reach England by sea. During that time, England had decided to stop restricting trading ships. The messages passed each other.**

➧ Since England controlled Canada, the Americans decided to invade but were quickly defeated. When they turned back to Detroit, the British pursued them and took over almost all of Michigan territory.

PEOPLE TO KNOW The Shawnee chief **TECUMSEH** sided with the British. In the 1812 battle for Detroit, his men wove in and out of the woods, making it seem like they were many more people.

THE BATTLES OF THE WAR OF 1812

STAT FACT **The Battle of Baltimore was in September 1814. America had 1,000 men and 20 guns. The British had 5,000 soldiers. Over two days, Baltimore's residents fought hard and successfully kept control of the city.**

PEOPLE TO KNOW **FRANCIS SCOTT KEY** was an American lawyer, held prisoner by the British during the battle of Baltimore. He wrote a poem about what he witnessed, which would later become the song "The Star-Spangled Banner."

In August 1814, British forces won the Battle of Bladensburg in Maryland and marched to Washington, DC. They burned public buildings, including the White House, which was then called the Executive Mansion.

The final battle of the War of 1812 took place in 1815. The Battle of New Orleans stopped the British from claiming US territory that was bought in the Louisiana Purchase.

★ **The war ended on January 15, 1815, when the Treaty of Ghent was signed by the British and the Americans. The peace treaty restored borders to where they were before the war. It was actually signed before the Battle of New Orleans, but the soldiers fighting the battle didn't know about it and hadn't realized the war was over.**

MOVING WEST ON THE OREGON TRAIL 1836–1870

After the Lewis and Clark expedition, traders and trappers had begun to move west. But it was mainly Christian and Mormon missionaries who led the way across America.

PEOPLE TO KNOW In 1836, newlyweds **MARCUS AND NARCISSA WHITMAN** made one of the first wagon crossings. Narcissa's letters about the trip encouraged families, women, and children to make the journey.

STAT FACT The Oregon Trail stretched **2,000 MILES** (3,200 kilometers) from Independence, Missouri, to Oregon City, Oregon. Hundreds of thousands of pioneers stocked their wagons to set out for new lives in the West.

TERM TO KNOW In 1843, Marcus Whitman led a **WAGON TRAIN** of more than 1,000 settlers. This was a group of people who moved together in covered wagons. This trip is now known as the "Great Emigration."

- People aimed to convert Indigenous Americans to Christianity as they traveled west. Their work was unsuccessful, and instead they brought many new diseases to the Indigenous Nations, just like early explorers did in the 15th and 16th centuries.

★ **The Oregon Trail wasn't one path. Pioneers traveled on different routes that branched in all directions through mountains and plains.**

LIFE ON THE OREGON TRAIL

➧ All along the trail, merchants created trading posts for settlers to buy supplies. The frontier became littered with garbage as the settlers used items and threw out what was broken.

STAT FACT **Only 80,000 of the more than 400,000 pioneers who traveled the trail settled in Oregon. Many made their way to California after 1848 when gold was found in Sutter Creek.**

★ **The journey along the trail took between four and six months. It was important to leave Missouri in April or May to avoid heavy winter snow.**

- The Indigenous American people and the pioneers had few conflicts. Mostly, the Indigenous Americans helped the pioneers. Since the pioneers were simply passing through, they traded goods and suggested good routes.

STAT FACT **Fort Laramie in Wyoming was a rest stop along the trail. People bought items and abandoned supplies they didn't need. In 1849, around 20,000 tons of bacon was left there.**

★ **Pioneers needed food that could last the long trip without spoiling. Potato cakes, oat cakes, and molasses cakes were popular. Buffalo jerky, pork and beans, and even chocolate were eaten during the journey.**

NATIVE AMERICAN REMOVAL AND TRAIL OF TEARS 1830–1850

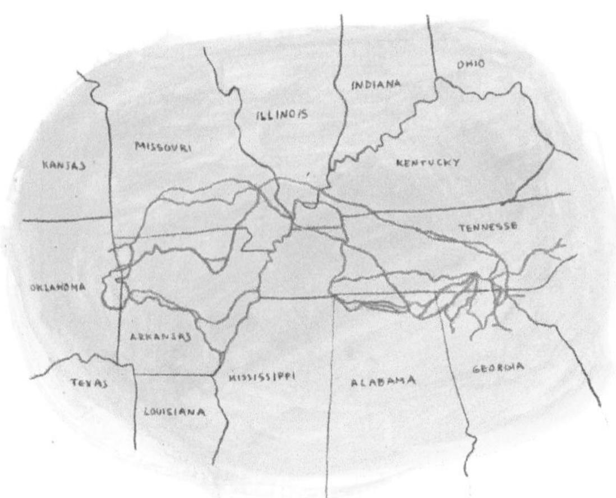

Route of the Trail of Tears

- In 1830, more than 125,000 Indigenous Americans lived in some Southern states. White settlers wanted their land to farm.

TERM TO KNOW The **INDIAN REMOVAL ACT** was signed by President Andrew Jackson in 1830. It said the president could take land from Indigenous Americans and give them land west of the Mississippi instead.

- In 1832, the Supreme Court ruled that the Cherokee in Georgia had rights to their land and the state couldn't make them leave. Jackson ignored the court and allowed Georgia to forcibly remove the Indigenous Nations.

STAT FACT **Between 1830 and 1850, the US government forced 100,000 Indigenous Americans to relocate to places they'd never lived before. The relocation was known as the Trail of Tears because of the hunger, disease, and death that occurred.**

- From 1830 to 1833, the Choctaw People were bound in chains and marched out of their homes in Mississippi. In 1836, the Creek People were forced to leave Georgia, Alabama, and Florida.

STAT FACT **Of the 15,000 Cherokee People who were forced to march to Oklahoma, 4,000 died on the journey.**

THE ALAMO

- From 1821, Texas was part of Mexico, but American settlers had made it their home. In December 1835, a small group of Texan-Americans took over a fort called the Alamo to claim Texas for the United States.

- General Sam Houston sent pioneer Jim Bowie to destroy the Alamo, which was in San Antonio, but Bowie decided to defend it instead. He ultimately died in the battle.

The dictator and general Antonio López de Santa Anna led the Mexicans to victory to win the Battle of the Alamo.

★ **The fighting blade called the Bowie knife is named for Jim Bowie.**

PEOPLE TO KNOW **DAVY CROCKETT**, an adventurer and politician, was known as the "King of the Wild Frontier." Crockett fought at the Alamo, but no one knows if he died or was captured.

STAT FACT About **200** Americans, and a few Mexican supporters, held out for **13** days before they lost the battle on March 6, 1836. "Remember the Alamo" became a slogan in the fight for Texas's independence from Mexico.

MANIFEST DESTINY

TERM TO KNOW **MANIFEST DESTINY** is the cultural and religious idea that God wanted America to stretch from the Atlantic to the Pacific Ocean. It includes false belief in the superiority of white Americans, which was used to justify removing Indigenous Americans.

- John O'Sullivan, a newspaper reporter, invented the phrase "Manifest Destiny" in 1845, but it wasn't a new idea. Europeans believed they were superior to the Indigenous people in the lands they colonized, too.

Manifest Destiny led to the expansion of settlements and the expulsion of cultures that were not Christian.

PEOPLE TO KNOW **JAMES POLK** became president in 1844. Driven by Manifest Destiny, he oversaw the annexation of more than a million square miles (over 1.6 million square kilometers), increasing the United States' territory from the Pacific Ocean to the Atlantic.

- A division grew in the nation between those who believed white Americans were culturally and racially superior, and those who did not. The country was heading toward civil war.

CHAPTER 6

A NATION DIVIDED

[1861–1865]

In the 1800s, tensions grew between the northern and southern regions of the United States. There were three main areas of disagreement: slavery, states' rights, and westward expansion. White Southerners enslaved people to work on their plantations, and the North felt that enslaving people was wrong. The southern states thought the federal government was taking away their rights. And as people continued to move west, new states could elect leaders who could change the rules. Debates turned to arguments and soon there would be armed conflict.

- **In 1820, Congress admitted Missouri to the United States as a slave state and Maine as a free state.**
- **The Kansas-Nebraska Act of 1854 allowed the settlers in each new state to determine their own rules on enslaving people.**
- **Abraham Lincoln was elected president in 1860, even though he wasn't on the ballot in 10 southern states because he was against slavery.**

TENSIONS BEFORE THE WAR

- Between 1854 and 1859, settlers in the territory of Kansas had differing beliefs about slavery, which led to conflict and violence. The period is called Bleeding Kansas.

- The Republican Party was formed in response to the Kansas-Nebraska Act. It was a new party opposed to the spread of slavery into the western states.

TERM TO KNOW **SECEDE** means to break off ties. In 1860, 11 southern states seceded, meaning they left the United States with the hope of forming their own independent country.

LIVES OF ENSLAVED PEOPLE

- Most enslaved people worked on large farms. They were assigned roles as house servants or field workers. Harsh punishments kept enslaved people from revolting or running away.

- Field workers lived in shacks and worked the farm. Domestic servants took care of children and attended to laundry, cleaning, and cooking, sometimes living in a small room of the house.

STAT FACT **In 1860, the price of an enslaved person depended on where the owner lived. An enslaved person cost $1,500 in Virginia or $1,800 in New Orleans. Overall, the average cost in the country was about $800 for an enslaved person.**

- Upon arrival to America, enslaved people were often intentionally separated from their family or community. This gave more power to the enslavers by further controlling and oppressing forced laborers.

TERM TO KNOW **SLAVE CODES** were laws in the South that said enslaved people couldn't own property, testify in court, or go anywhere without permission. Enslaved people could be prizes in raffles or given as gifts.

- Many enslaved people created their own religious traditions with a mix of Christianity and their own faiths from Africa. Song and prayer helped enslaved people bear the daily trauma of their suffering.

ABOLITIONISM

TERM TO KNOW The **ABOLITIONIST MOVEMENT** was the organized effort to end enslavement throughout the United States. Inspired by religious beliefs, it became a political movement that increased tensions in the divided country.

PEOPLE TO KNOW **ELIZABETH CADY STANTON** was an abolitionist. She gathered other women who shared her politics and together they fought against enslavement and for women's rights.

- The Philadelphia Female Anti-Slavery Society was founded in 1833. Lucretia Mott, one of the founders, wanted women to speak out. She was criticized for not behaving as a "proper woman."

Elizabeth Cady Stanton

In 1840, men from around the world gathered in London for the World Anti-Slavery Convention. Their goal was to end all enslavement.

PEOPLE TO KNOW **WILLIAM LLOYD GARRISON** ran an anti-slavery newspaper called *The Liberator*. When he started the paper in 1831, he argued that freed enslaved people would integrate and contribute greatly to society.

- A Protestant religious movement called the Second Great Awakening helped promote the idea that all men were equal in the eyes of God. This religious belief helped spread Abolitionist principles.

UNDERGROUND RAILROAD

- The Underground Railroad was a secret system in the early 1800s. Moving from private homes to hideouts, enslaved people would make their way north to places where they'd become free.

TERM TO KNOW Train terminology was used in the Underground Railroad. **CONDUCTORS** were the people who helped the enslaved fugitives travel north. Homes and hideouts were called **STATIONS** and **DEPOTS**. **STOCKHOLDERS** provided money to keep the system running.

★ **The Levi Coffin House in Indiana was a stopping point for thousands of slaves. The house had secret rooms. A grain wagon included a hiding area.**

PEOPLE TO KNOW **HARRIET TUBMAN** escaped through the Underground Railroad and achieved her freedom before helping others as a nurse, conductor, and spy. Between 1850 and 1860, she made 19 trips, leading hundreds of enslaved people to freedom.

- It could take as many as six weeks to travel to a safe place on the Underground Railroad. People traveled at night, mostly by foot, and carried very few belongings.

PEOPLE TO KNOW **FREDERICK DOUGLASS** escaped slavery and became a leader in the Abolitionist movement. He used the Underground Railroad himself, then hid about 400 people in his New York home during their own escapes.

DRED SCOTT AND THE FUGITIVE SLAVE ACT

PEOPLE TO KNOW **DRED SCOTT** was born into slavery. After living with his owner in free states and territories, Missouri law said he could be free. In 1846, Scott and his wife, Harriet, sued the woman who owned them after she refused to grant their freedom.

- In 1850, the Scotts won their case and were free. But in 1852, a Missouri court overturned local law and enslaved them again. In 1856, the case went to the United States Supreme Court.

The Supreme Court declared the Scotts had to remain enslaved. They were sold again, but the newest enslaver freed them.

- The Fugitive Slave Act of 1793 permitted local governments to arrest enslaved people who escaped and send them back to their enslavers. The law also punished anyone who helped those who escaped.

The Fugitive Slave Act was expanded to include stronger punishments in 1850 because southern states felt it wasn't being adequately enforced.

- After 1850, it was too risky for enslaved people to stop in northern states. Enslaved people began heading directly for Canada, where the Fugitive Slave Act was not valid.

JOHN BROWN

PEOPLE TO KNOW **JOHN BROWN** was a white abolitionist who wanted to start a revolt with enslaved people. He felt that Black people needed to work together with white people in armed conflict for freedom.

- In October 1859, John Brown and his men raided the federal armory in Harpers Ferry, Virginia. The plan was to get the guns and give them to enslaved people for a rebellion.

- The enslaved people who raided Harpers Ferry were captured or killed. John Brown was sentenced to death for treason against the state of Virginia, murder, and insurrection.

ABOLITIONIST PUBLICATIONS

STAT FACT **In the 1850s, about 20,000 enslaved people made it to Canada. After escaping to Canada, Henry Bibb began publishing *Voice of the Fugitive*, a newspaper that helped enslaved people find their families.**

Mary Ann Shadd Cary was born free in Delaware. She founded *The Provincial Freeman*, Canada's first anti-slavery newspaper, in 1853.

Sojourner Truth was an American abolitionist and advocate of women's rights. Born into slavery, she was sold four times. A white family bought her freedom for $25. She dictated her autobiography in 1850.

Mary Ann Shadd Cary

ABRAHAM LINCOLN AND SLAVERY

- Abraham Lincoln lost five elections before becoming president in 1861. In the months before he was inaugurated, seven southern states seceded to form the Confederate States of America.

★ **Abraham Lincoln's wife, Mary Todd, came from a family of slaveholders. Her brother and half-brothers served in the Confederate Army. Mary Todd's own feelings about slavery are unclear.**

- On March 11, 1861, the Constitution of the Confederate States of America was adopted for 13 southern states. The constitution permitted slavery but prohibited the trade of enslaved people from Africa.

- Lincoln did not believe Black people deserved all the same rights as white people. However, he did believe that all people should be rewarded for their work, which meant slavery was wrong.

- For a long time, Lincoln believed the answer to slavery was for Black people to leave and settle in Africa or Central America. He wasn't sure Black and white people could live together.

- Once war broke out between the North and the South, Lincoln declared that enslaved people had to be freed, although he believed it needed to happen gradually.

THE CIVIL WAR

- In April 1861, Confederate soldiers attacked Union forces at Fort Sumter, South Carolina, marking the beginning of the Civil War. In July, Lincoln asked Congress for 500,000 troops. It was clear the war was going to be long.

Civil War uniforms

- The First Battle of Bull Run in July 1861 was the first major battle of the Civil War. The Confederate Army beat the Union Army, though both sides suffered great losses.

★ **Soldiers didn't fight in battles every day. In their downtime they wrote letters home, wrestled, played checkers and chess, and sang songs.**

★ When provisions were low, soldiers were known to trade with the enemy. Confederate soldiers liked coffee and newspapers, which they exchanged with Union soldiers for tobacco.

STAT FACT There were more than **10,000** armed conflicts during the war. An estimated **620,000** people died. The bloodiest single day was on September 17, 1862, at the Battle of Antietam. About **23,000** men were killed, wounded, or went missing that day.

PEOPLE TO KNOW The Union victory at the Battle of Gettysburg in 1863 was a turning point in the war. The Civil War ended when the Confederate Army surrendered on April 9, 1865.

The Confederate Army (left) surrendered on April 9, 1865, to the Union Army (right).

CIVIL WAR LEADERS

PEOPLE TO KNOW **JEFFERSON DAVIS** was the president of the Confederate States. He was a US senator from Mississippi and had a farm with enslaved workers. In 1865, he was captured and charged with treason, but he was never convicted.

PEOPLE TO KNOW **ROBERT E. LEE** was the general in charge of the Confederate troops. Lee surrendered to Ulysses S. Grant, the commander of the Union Army, to end the Civil War.

PEOPLE TO KNOW **ROSE GREENHOW** was a Confederate spy. She hosted events for Union politicians and passed information to the Confederate forces. Her delivery of an important coded message helped the Confederacy win the First Battle of Bull Run.

This Civil War cipher might have been used by spies like Rose Greenhow.

PEOPLE TO KNOW **ABRAHAM GALLOWAY** was an enslaved man who escaped the South. He returned to recruit Black volunteers for the Union Army. In 1868, Galloway was elected to the North Carolina State Senate.

PEOPLE TO KNOW **CLARA BARTON** was a nurse to Union soldiers during the war. She'd go to the battlefields to help. In 1881, Barton founded the American Red Cross.

PEOPLE TO KNOW In 1865, **ULYSSES S. GRANT** led Union troops to victory in Vicksburg, Virginia, and Chattanooga, Tennessee. Grant became the 18th president of the United States in 1869.

EMANCIPATION PROCLAMATION

TERM TO KNOW The Emancipation Proclamation that Lincoln issued on January 1, 1863, was an important step toward the abolition of slavery. **EMANCIPATION** means to free someone from slavery, and a **PROCLAMATION** is an official announcement.

- The Emancipation Proclamation declared that all enslaved people were freed, but it didn't apply to border states that were with the Union. It only applied to states that had seceded from the Union.

TERM TO KNOW A **FUGITIVE SLAVE** is an enslaved person who escaped slavery around the time of the Civil War. Some historians estimate that about 100,000 enslaved people attempted to free themselves by escaping to free states or territories.

- Even after the Emancipation Proclamation was issued, fighting continued in the Civil War. The news didn't reach Texas for two years. The last enslaved people were freed on June 19, 1865, now a federal holiday called Juneteenth.

- Indigenous Americans fought on both sides of the war. Some even enslaved people in the South. In 1863, the Cherokee issued their own Emancipation Proclamation, declaring freedom for enslaved people.

- Slavery was finally abolished throughout the United States with the 13th Amendment to the Constitution on December 6, 1865.

More than 100,000 formerly enslaved people fought for the Union.

CHAPTER 7

RECONSTRUCTION

[1863-1877]

After the Civil War, 4 million freed people needed to build new lives. The Confederate states, still reeling from their loss in the war, had to be brought back into the United States. Amid these turbulent shifts, President Lincoln was assassinated in 1865. The new president, Andrew Johnson, let the southern states pass laws that restricted the freedom of formerly enslaved people. Although life for Black Americans was improved in some areas, in many others, a rise in extremism would prolong their struggles.

- **Reconstruction was the effort to integrate formerly enslaved people into society, while also reintegrating the Confederate states.**
- **After the Civil War, Lincoln wanted Southerners to pledge an oath to the Union. His plan was to forgive the Confederacy and move on to reunification.**
- **In 1865, Abraham Lincoln was shot and killed while watching a play. He never got the chance to finalize Reconstruction. That duty fell to President Andrew Johnson, a Confederate sympathizer.**

PRESIDENT JOHNSON AND RECONSTRUCTION

- In 1865 and 1866, many southern states enacted "Black Codes." These laws pushed many formerly enslaved people back into forced labor.

PEOPLE TO KNOW Union General **WILLIAM T. SHERMAN** created an order that set aside land on the southeast coast, on which newly freed people would be given a 40-acre plot. President Johnson reversed the order.

TERM TO KNOW **IMPEACHMENT** is when Congress charges the president with misconduct. In 1868, President Johnson vetoed Congress's plan for Reconstruction, then was impeached when he fired his secretary of war.

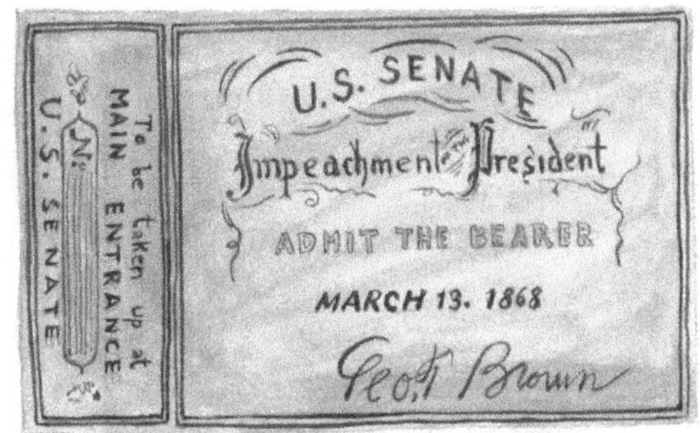

THE 13TH, 14TH, AND 15TH AMENDMENTS

- The 13th Amendment to the Constitution abolished slavery within the United States and its territories.

TERM TO KNOW **RATIFY** means to accept. The state of Mississippi did not ratify the 13th Amendment until 1995.

- The 14th Amendment provided citizenship to people who had formerly been enslaved, granting "equal protection under the law" to all citizens of the United States.

TERM TO KNOW The Supreme Court case of *Plessy v. Ferguson* in 1896 defined what equal protection meant in the 14th Amendment. It was called "separate but equal," which allowed for **RACIAL SEGREGATION**. This is the practice of separating people based on race or ethnicity in daily life.

- The 15th Amendment gave African American men the right to vote. Despite this, many southern states found ways to prevent this right, like making Black men pay a fee to vote that was not applied to white people.

When the 15th Amendment was ratified in 1870, Levi Coffin, who worked on the Underground Railroad said, "Our work is done."

- Even though enslaved people were freed, enslavement was still allowed as punishment for certain crimes.

POSTWAR POLITICS

- The Reconstruction Acts of 1867 divided the South into five military districts, gave freedmen and white men the right to vote, and required states to ratify the 14th Amendment.

STAT FACT **For the first time, Black people could run for elected office. Between 1867 and 1877, there were TWO Black senators, 14 Black members of the House of Representatives, and nearly 800 Black elected officials in southern states.**

PEOPLE TO KNOW **ROBERT SMALLS** was a formerly enslaved man from Charleston, South Carolina, who helped 17 people escape slavery. In 1874, he was elected to the House of Representatives.

TERM TO KNOW **CARPETBAGGERS** were Northerners who moved to the South. While some went to help rebuild the South, others were greedy people seeking to get rich for their own gain under the guise of Reconstruction.

TERM TO KNOW A **SCALAWAG** was a southern person who helped northern Republicans during Reconstruction. It was an insult used by southern white Republicans to describe other Southerners who they thought were betraying them.

- In 1870, Hiram Revels was the first Black person to serve in the Senate. Blanche Kelso Bruce was the second in 1875. Ninety-two years later, the third Black senator was Edward Brooke of Massachusetts in 1966.

GENERAL IMPACT OF RECONSTRUCTION

Reconstruction-Era advertisement

- The Civil Rights Act of 1875 gave additional rights to African Americans by banning segregation in public places like hotels and theaters.

- After Reconstruction, southern states rolled back the rights given to Black people under the Constitution. In 1883, the Supreme Court said the Civil Rights Act was unconstitutional, and segregation was revived.

- Hate groups, like the Ku Klux Klan, were formed in the South and falsely believe in the superiority of white people over others. For more than 150 years, these groups have attacked Black people and Civil Rights advocates.

STAT FACT **An economic depression in 1873 happened toward the end of Reconstruction. About 15,000 businesses closed and many people didn't have jobs.**

- In 1872, the Republican Party began to split. Radical Republicans believed that the South should have been punished for the war. Other Republicans felt that Reconstruction was successful and wanted to move on.

TERM TO KNOW Farmers and laborers, many of whom were once enslaved, rented plots of land from landowners to grow crops in a practice called **SHARECROPPING.**

WOMEN AND RECONSTRUCTION

TERM TO KNOW **SUFFRAGE** is the right to vote. The 15th Amendment did not guarantee suffrage for women. Women who had been working hard for voting rights, called **SUFFRAGISTS**, felt betrayed.

- During the war, many women took over and ran their family businesses since men were fighting. Women worked as journalists and ran newspapers. Educational opportunities were rising, and women wanted more political influence.

- Black women led the reunification of enslaved families. Ads were placed in newspapers, and a network was created to try to find people who had been separated during slavery.

TERM TO KNOW In 1869, the National Woman Suffrage Association opposed the 15th Amendment and wanted women to be included. That year, the more popular American Women's Suffrage Association focused on voting rights for women.

PEOPLE TO KNOW The suffragist **SUSAN B. ANTHONY** was angry that the 15th Amendment didn't give women the right to vote. In 1872, she voted and was arrested. After her release, she traveled around the country trying to change the law.

PEOPLE TO KNOW **MARY CHURCH TERRELL** was a college-educated African American woman who worked to promote racial equality and women's right to vote.

THE COMPROMISE OF 1877

- In 1876, the Republican Rutherford B. Hayes was running for the presidency against the Democrat Samuel J. Tilden. The winner in South Carolina, Louisiana, and Florida was unclear, so Congress had to step in to decide who won.

★ **The Compromise of 1877 was a resolution made by both Democratic and Republican members of Congress that gave Hayes the presidency.**

- The Compromise stated that Democrats would respect the rights of Black Americans. It also required Hayes to withdraw federal troops from the South, give federal funding for a new railroad, and appoint a Southerner to his cabinet.

★ **When Hayes was elected president it angered northern Democrats, who suspected election fraud. They called him "His Fraudulency."**

★ **The Compromise promised the construction of a transcontinental railroad through the southern states, much like the one that already existed in the North. But this never happened.**

- After troops were removed from the South, the Democrats went back on their promise to protect the political and civil rights of African Americans. They instead created laws for racial separation.

JIM CROW LAWS

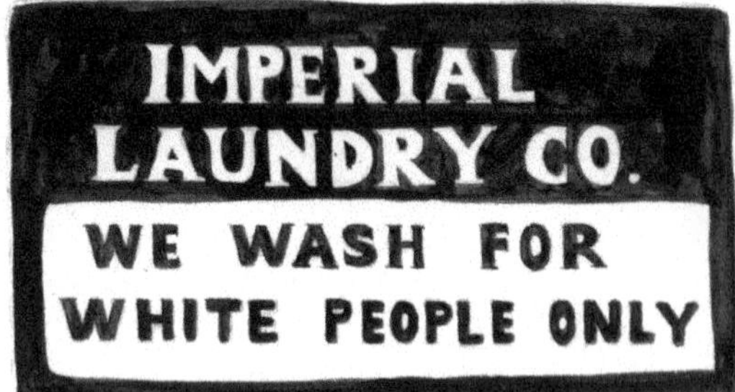

- Beginning in the 1880s and extending through the 1960s, Jim Crow laws enforced segregation throughout the United States. Different states had their own laws.

- Jim Crow laws were named after a stereotypical Black character in a minstrel show. Minstrel shows were racist plays in which a white man wearing black makeup would act like an awkward, uneducated enslaved man for entertainment.

★ **Jim Crow laws in Georgia said that a Black barber couldn't cut a white woman's hair, and that Black baseball teams had to play two blocks away from white teams.**

TERM TO KNOW The Ku Klux Klan formed in 1865 as a violent group that believed in **WHITE SUPREMACY**. This is a false belief that white people are better than other people. Some members of the Ku Klux Klan served in government and law enforcement, where they had power to enact racist laws.

★ In Alabama, bus stations had separate waiting rooms and ticket windows for Black riders and white riders. In North Carolina, schoolbooks that were used by Black students couldn't be used by white people.

STAT FACT In Louisiana, there were about **130,000** Black registered voters in 1896, but due to the reversal of the Civil Rights act, fear, and intimidation, that number was **1,342** by 1904.

IMPACT OF SEGREGATION

- Public transport was a significant part of segregation in the South. Being forced to sit in a different part of the bus, or take a different bus altogether, was a daily psychological strain and reminder to Black people that the law saw them as inferior to white people.

Black Southerners had a higher illness and death rate because there were fewer doctors and hospitals available to them.

TERM TO KNOW **UNIONS** are labor organizations that represent workers in negotiations with businesses to help improve wages and working conditions. Black workers weren't allowed to join unions, so they had poorer job opportunities.

- Throughout the South, separate schools were established for black children. These schools were often poorly funded compared to the white schools.

TERM TO KNOW **MISCEGENATION LAWS** were rules that forbade Black people and white people to marry each other under threat of punishment. Predominantly passed in the South in the 1800s, by 1900 these laws had spread widely to the North as well.

CHAPTER 8

RESHAPING A NATION

[1860–1914]

The late 1800s to the early 1900s was a time of great creativity and innovation. New inventions made life easier, but since not everyone had money or access to them, the gap between rich and poor grew. New cities emerged in the west, which also led to new conflicts with those who had been on the land for generations. After an economic depression in the 1890s, companies combined resources and developed groundbreaking technologies. And there was a war on the horizon that would draw in the entire world.

- **Kodak introduced a camera in 1900. Sold for a dollar, it was the first camera that allowed amateurs to take their own photos.**
- **The first narrative silent film, *The Great Train Robbery*, debuted in 1903.**
- **The National Association for the Advancement of Colored People (NAACP) was founded in 1909 in response to violence against African Americans.**

SETTLEMENTS IN THE WEST

➧ During the Civil War, in 1862, President Lincoln signed the Homestead Act, which encouraged western settlement by giving settlers land to farm.

★ In 1882, Jewish immigrants from Russia settled in Cotopaxi, Colorado. The colony ultimately failed because the land in the Rocky Mountains was too difficult to farm.

➧ African Americans were moving west. More than 1,200 towns, like Boley, Oklahoma, founded in 1903, were all-Black settlements.

TRANSCONTINENTAL RAILROAD

PEOPLE TO KNOW In the 1850s, civil engineer **THEODORE JUDAH** had the idea for a railroad from the East Coast to California. The plan was so wildly ambitious, people called him "Crazy Judah."

- The Central Pacific Railroad Company started construction in 1863 from the west, and the Union Pacific Railroad Company started in 1866 from the east. The western crew had to blast through mountains. The eastern crew moved quickly through the plains.

★ **In 1865, Central Pacific hired Chinese workers, many who had come for the Gold Rush. The Union Pacific workers were mostly Irish immigrants and Civil War veterans.**

- Union Pacific laborers were occasionally attacked by Indigenous tribes who were frustrated that the railroad was ruining their lands. They'd sometimes destroy the tracks or steal the workers' livestock, but they were unsuccessful in stopping the trains.

- In 1869, the transcontinental railroad became reality when the Union Pacific railroad met the Central Pacific railroad in Promontory, Utah. A telegraph message was sent around the country that said "Done."

★ **The final spike in the track was made of gold. The spike was driven in by a railroad worker and later swapped out for iron.**

COWBOY LIFE

As selling cattle became an important way for Westerners to earn money, cowboys were needed to herd the cattle and move them from place to place.

TERM TO KNOW **VAQUEROS** were Mexican cowboys. Known for roping and riding, they were hired in the West to work the ranches. Settlers learned from the vaqueros and adopted their style.

Cowpoke, buckaroo, cowhand, and cowpuncher were all nicknames for cowboys.

PEOPLE TO KNOW **CHARLES GOODNIGHT** was a famous rancher in Texas. There is a trail named after him between Texas and Colorado where he once drove cattle. He also invented the chuckwagon, a portable kitchen.

★ **Cowboys often wore the same clothing for weeks without changing or washing. Leather leggings called chaps helped protect their legs from thorns, and special hats protected their eyes in the sun.**

- One in four of the original cowboys in the West was a freed enslaved person, including Bill Pickett, a famous cowboy who competed in rodeo shows. He is credited with inventing steer wrestling.

FORCED CHANGES IN INDIGENOUS AMERICAN LIFE

- When the 14th Amendment gave African American men the right to vote in 1868, Indigenous American men were mostly left out. They were seen as an independent nation rather than citizens of the United States.

- The Dawes Act of 1887 gave Indigenous Americans individual plots of land. It was hoped that families would become farmers like other white settlers, but the farmland they were given was bad and divided tribal lands.

White settlers were killing bison by the thousands. Indigenous Americans historically relied on bison for food and other products.

PEOPLE TO KNOW **GERONIMO** was a fearless Apache leader who refused to leave his tribal land. When he was forced to a reservation in Arizona, he escaped repeatedly and was chased by US and Mexican military.

TERM TO KNOW **ASSIMILATION** is when a minority group is made to adopt the values of a dominant culture. From 1860 to 1978, Indigenous American children were forced to attend government-run boarding schools designed to make them assimilate and abandon their own traditions.

Geronimo

In 1879, Colonel Richard Henry Pratt opened an assimilation school in Pennsylvania. There were 150 similar schools open nationwide.

MAJOR INVENTIONS

★ **The first successful typewriter was patented in 1868 by Christopher Latham Sholes. The layout of its keys, known as the QWERTY keyboard, is still used today.**

- In 1876, Alexander Graham Bell discovered a way to convert a voice into electrical impulses then back again, so the voice could be heard over a distance. This invention became the telephone.

Bell's telephone

- In 1879, Thomas Edison patented the first incandescent light bulb. On his team was Lewis Latimer, an African American who created a way to stop the glass bulb from breaking.

In 1886, Josephine Cochrane invented the dishwasher. She sold them to hotels and at the World's Fair.

PEOPLE TO KNOW **MADAM C. J. WALKER** was the first female self-made millionaire. Starting in 1907, she began designing and selling hair products for Black women called the Walker System.

Henry Ford's Model T car was manufactured beginning in 1908. This was one of the first affordable, mass-produced vehicles. Ford is also credited with inventing the assembly line that made manufacturing more efficient.

★ In 1886, John Pemberton invented the flavor syrup called Coca-Cola. Original Coca-Cola barrels were painted red so no one would confuse them with barrels of alcohol.

★ Nintendo made popular card games in Japan in the late 1800s, and in 1902, the company brought its games to the United States. As local demand for international imports grew, the company was a pioneer in keeping up with technological changes.

PEOPLE TO KNOW **GEORGE WASHINGTON CARVER** was born into slavery, but as a freeman sought an education in agricultural science. He is credited with creating more than 300 different products from peanuts.

- William K. L. Dickson had ideas that gave birth to the motion picture. Together with Thomas Edison in 1892, he worked on the kinetoscope, a camera where images seen through a peephole appeared to be moving.

PEOPLE TO KNOW **WILBUR AND ORVILLE WRIGHT** were bicycle makers who liked experimenting with glider planes. In 1903, the plane they created lifted off, making history as the first aircraft flight.

THE SPANISH-AMERICAN WAR

- The Spanish-American War was Cuba's fight for independence from Spain. It began on April 25, 1898, and lasted about three months.

- The American battleship USS *Maine* exploded and sank in a Cuban harbor on February 15, 1898, killing 260 men. This encouraged the United States to join the war, supporting Cuba.

★ **To this day, no one knows who blew up the *Maine*. Although the Spanish were blamed, the explosion may have simply been an accident.**

STAT FACT **Led by Commander George Dewey, the United States attacked the Spanish fleet at Manila Bay in the Philippines. FOUR HUNDRED Spanish sailors were killed and 10 ships destroyed. The Battle of Manila Bay was a US victory.**

- In December 1898, the Spanish-American War ended, and the United States was granted several new overseas territories that were previously claimed by Spain, including the Philippines, Guam, and Puerto Rico. Cuba became a US protectorate.

Today, Puerto Rico is still a US territory.

IMMIGRATION TO AMERICA

STAT FACT Between 1881 and 1920, more than **20 MILLION** immigrants from all over the world came to America. As more people came, racist and anti-immigrant groups grew in power and looked for ways to stop more newcomers.

➧ In the mid–19th century, famine in Ireland sent people looking for new homes. Between 1820 and 1930, nearly 4.5 million Irish people immigrated to America. Most newcomers came in through New York.

★ **In 1886, France gave the Statue of Liberty to the United States as a gift. Standing in New York Harbor, she was a symbol welcoming new immigrants to the country.**

The Statue of Liberty

- Chinese immigrants who had come for the Gold Rush and to work on the railroad faced racism. In 1882, the United States halted all immigration from China. From 1902 to 1943, immigrating from China was illegal.

STAT FACT **Nearly 5 MILLION German people came to the United States in the late 1800s.**

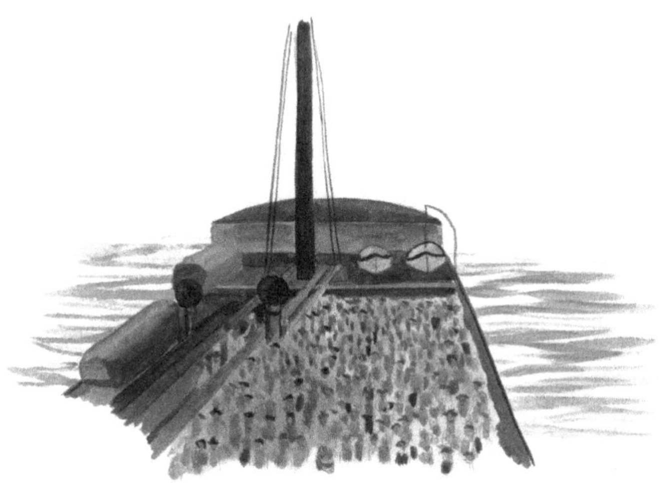

Between 1820 and 1880, Jewish people facing antisemitic violence in Germany and Austria-Hungary created communities in the United States.

THE PROGRESSIVE ERA AND NEW PROTECTIVE LAWS

TERM TO KNOW **PROGRESSIVE** refers to new ideas, or people who advocate for social change. In the 1900s, immigration, industrialization, and politics led to a Progressive Era of reform.

- In March 1911, there was a fire at the Triangle Shirtwaist Factory in New York City that killed 145 workers. This tragedy brought awareness of unsafe factory conditions. Laws and regulations were passed to protect workers.

In 1913, the 17th Amendment to the Constitution gave voters the right to choose their Senate representatives from each state.

- The Sherman Antitrust Act of 1890 made it illegal to limit business competition. This was meant to make things fairer for consumers and smaller businesses.

- The Keating-Owen Act of 1916 created rules for factories and mines that used child labor. The goal was to stop factories hiring children under 14 years old, mine workers under 16 years old, and to reduce work hours.

★ **Progressives were also concerned about the environment. John Muir was a scientist and influential writer who fought to protect animals and natural lands by setting some areas off-limits for construction and development.**

John Muir spent a lot of time in Yosemite National Park.

CHAPTER 9

EARLY TO MIDDLE 20TH CENTURY

[1914–1968]

By the time America entered World War I, the country was an established global power. The nation stretched from the East Coast to the West Coast. Settlers had become farmers and cities were growing quickly. Steel was a top commodity. The mass production of cars, telephones, and radios brought people together in new ways. New wealth brought art, architecture, and cultural change. This was a time of progressive reform, bold ideas, innovation, and patriotism.

- **In the 1880s, John D. Rockefeller controlled 90 percent of the oil refineries and pipelines in the United States. By 1916, he was the world's first billionaire.**
- **Juliette Gordon Low founded the Girl Scouts in 1912. Low felt that opportunities were needed for girls to come together and build strong character.**
- **In 1918, the world suffered a flu pandemic, and about 675,000 people died in the United States.**

WORLD WAR I 1914–1918

TERM TO KNOW The **ALLIES** were the combination of forces from France, Russia, Belgium, the British Empire, and the United States that fought together in World War I. The **CENTRAL POWERS** were Germany, Austria, Hungary, Bulgaria, and Turkey.

- For three years, President Woodrow Wilson tried to avoid entering the war. In April 1917, he was angry that the Germans were targeting US ships and asked Congress to declare war on Germany.

STAT FACT **Machine guns, tanks, naval boats, and airplanes were used in the war, ushering in a new way of fighting. Germany surrendered November 11, 1918. The total war casualties are estimated at 37.5 MILLION people.**

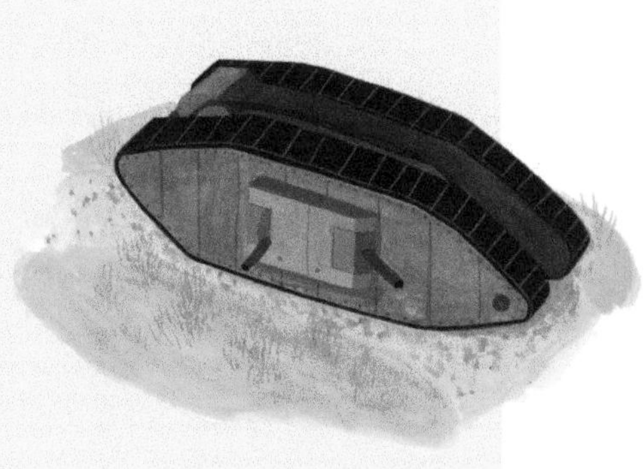

ROARING TWENTIES

The Roaring Twenties were called that because it was a decade of improved wealth and social freedoms for many. Moral standards were challenged, and so were dated belief systems.

★ **Convenient packaged foods became popular. Candy bars, peanut butter, sliced bread, fruit punch, and frozen food were often made with preservatives, allowing foods to stay fresh longer.**

STAT FACT **Industry and technology led to bold new architecture. In New York City, the Empire State Building was the tallest building ever built at the time. Finished in 1931, it was 1,250 FEET (381 meters) high.**

- The Scopes Trial in 1925 was the prosecution of a science teacher, John Scopes, for teaching the theory of evolution in a Tennessee public school. The case reflected conflicting ideas about science and religion at the time.

TERM TO KNOW **FLAPPERS** were women who challenged traditional ideas of womanhood. They wore short dresses and were often seen dancing and drinking. They were both criticized and admired for their independence.

- From 1920 to 1933, the sale of alcohol was forbidden. This era, called Prohibition, led to a large illegal network of alcohol sales, hidden bars, and the rise of gang violence.

WOMEN'S RIGHTS

In 1919, the 19th Amendment gave women the right to vote. In 1920, women could vote for the first time.

- Advertisers used images of women driving cars and smoking to show them as free and fashionable. As manufacturing made this lifestyle more affordable, this idea of beauty began to take hold.

- The lure of office work attracted many women in the 1920s. A spike in typing, filing, and general secretarial jobs allowed more women to work outside of the home.

★ **Women wanted the freedom to wear what they wanted, even while swimming. A one-piece suit showed more of the neck, legs, and arms than before, and women were arrested for the crime of showing too much skin.**

PEOPLE TO KNOW Women began running for office. In 1920, **EVA HAMILTON** became the first woman elected to the Michigan Senate. In New Mexico in 1923, Soledad Chacón was the first Latina, and woman of color, to hold statewide elected office.

HARLEM RENAISSANCE

- By the beginning of the 20th century, hundreds of thousands of Black people were leaving the South. Many relocated to cities like Chicago, New York, Detroit, and Los Angeles.

STAT FACT The Harlem section of New York City was a white neighborhood before 1920 when 175,000 African Americans settled there. They found work, built communities, and sparked an artistic awakening known as the Harlem Renaissance.

PEOPLE TO KNOW Performer **JOSEPHINE BAKER**, known for her talent and fun costumes, refused to perform for segregated audiences. She had great comedy skills, starred in two movies, and was a top-paid entertainer.

The Cotton Club, Harlem

PEOPLE TO KNOW **W.E.B. DU BOIS** was an intellectual and activist who cofounded the National Association for the Advancement of Colored People (NAACP).

PEOPLE TO KNOW Writer **ZORA NEALE HURSTON** shared the experiences of Black women in her plays, short stories, and novels. She is regarded as one of the greatest writers of the 20th century.

PEOPLE TO KNOW Musician **DUKE ELLINGTON** was a jazz performer, composer, and band leader. In 1923, he moved to Harlem, played regularly at famed nightclub the Cotton Club, and gained worldwide acclaim.

GREAT DEPRESSION

- The stock market plummeted several times in October 1929. The worst stock market crash in US history, called Black Tuesday, took place on October 29. On that day, the market lost $14 billion.

STAT FACT **About 11,000 banks failed and shut down after the stock market crash. One out of every four people was out of work, and hundreds of thousands of people were evicted from their homes.**

TERM TO KNOW Many people blamed President Herbert Hoover for the unemployment and homelessness. Shantytowns, where people built and lived in shacks after losing their homes, were called **HOOVERVILLES**.

- In the Southern Plains and the Midwest, dry, dusty winds blew away topsoil needed for farming. These dust storms carried soil as far as Washington, DC. The worst storm was in 1935 in the Oklahoma panhandle.

- In 1933, Franklin D. Roosevelt became president. He created a series of programs called the New Deal that helped regulate the stock market and banks and create more jobs.

The Great Depression ended with the start of World War II, since going to war required new industry and jobs.

WORLD WAR II 1939–1945

In 1939, the German Chancellor Adolf Hitler sent his troops into Poland. Great Britain and France declared war on Germany.

STAT FACT **Between 1939 and 1945, 45 to 60 MILLION people were killed in World War II, including 6 MILLION Jews that Hitler's Nazi party targeted and murdered.**

On December 7, 1941, the Japanese attacked the US naval base at Pearl Harbor in Hawaii, killing 2,403 servicemen and injuring many more. America entered the war, and in 1945, dropped two nuclear bombs on the Japanese cities of Hiroshima and Nagasaki, instantly killing 120,000 people.

PEOPLE TO KNOW **JEANNETTE RANKIN** was the first woman elected to Congress. As a lifelong pacifist, she was the only person to vote against America entering World War I.

★ **Rosie the Riveter was the image of a woman saying "We Can Do It!" working to help the war effort. The ad campaign was meant to encourage temporary work during the war, but women continued to stay in the workforce after the war.**

- D-Day, which signaled the near-end of the war, was June 6, 1944. On that day, 156,000 British, Canadian, and American troops came ashore in France's Normandy region to fight the Germans.

CHANGE MAKERS

PEOPLE TO KNOW **BETTY FRIEDAN** was one of the early leaders of the women's rights movement in the 1960s. Her book *The Feminine Mystique* was an inspirational text for women who wanted to work outside the home.

- Folk music used poetic lyrics to share feelings about common people and politics. Musicians like Bob Dylan and Joan Baez brought folk music and songs of political protest to the mainstream.

PEOPLE TO KNOW In 1965, **CESAR CHAVEZ**, an activist who fought for the rights of farmworkers, led a successful strike against California's grape growers for better pay and working conditions. His lifetime of work as a labor leader was recognized with a Presidential Medal of Freedom in 1994.

PEOPLE TO KNOW **ANDY WARHOL** was an artist who used images of famous people, comic strips, and everyday objects to examine life in the 1960s. His mass-produced work was designed to make art accessible and relatable to all people, not just the elite.

★ **Walt Disney arrived in California in 1923. After building success with animated films, he opened the Disneyland amusement park in 1955.**

On July 20, 1969, Neil Armstrong and Edwin "Buzz" Aldrin became the first people to step on the Moon.

CIVIL RIGHTS MOVEMENT

- In the 1950s and 1960s, the civil rights movement mobilized different people from all over the country to fight for equality and end discrimination against Black Americans.

- In 1954, the Supreme Court ruled in *Brown v. the Board of Education* that segregation in schools was illegal. It wasn't until 1957 that nine Black children desegregated an Arkansas high school, with federal troops escorting their entry.

PEOPLE TO KNOW **REVEREND DR. MARTIN LUTHER KING JR.** was a civil rights and anti-segregation leader. He organized protests and staged a massive march for justice in Washington, DC. His influential work changed race relations forever.

PEOPLE TO KNOW **MALCOLM X** was a civil rights leader who believed that Black people should protect themselves "by any means necessary." His ideas often clashed with those of Martin Luther King Jr., who preached nonviolence.

- In 1965, there were three planned protest marches from Selma to Montgomery, Alabama. The second march was called Bloody Sunday because law officials beat back the protestors, injuring 60 people.

- On the third march from Selma to Montgomery, Martin Luther King Jr. was joined by religious leaders from different faiths. Rabbi Abraham Joshua Heschel said, "I prayed with my feet."

Reverend Dr. Martin Luther King Jr. speaking at the March on Washington, August 28, 1963.

CHAPTER 10

HIGHLIGHTS OF MODERN AMERICA

[1970 to today]

The Civil Rights Act was signed in 1964, prohibiting discrimination based on race, color, religion, sex, or national origin. Though more work remains to be done, the years of Jim Crow laws officially ended. The decades that followed would see other forms of discrimination, but they would also pave the way for America's first Black president. Rights for women and immigrants and protections for the environment were activist causes, as were preventing future wars, individual gun ownership rights, and defenses of free speech. Phones, computers, and the Internet brought exciting technologies and challenges.

- **In 1971, the 26th Amendment lowered the voting age from 21 to 18.**
- **The movie *Star Wars* was released on May 25, 1977.**
- **In 1995, Amazon and eBay launched websites. Consumers spent about 861.12 billion dollars with merchants online in 2020.**

COMPUTERS AND THE INTERNET

- ARPANET was an early network that set the foundation for the Internet. In 1973, people in England and Norway connected to the system, ushering in a new era of global networking.

★ **Teenagers Bill Gates and Paul Allen got caught hacking their school's computer system. Instead of punishment, they were asked to improve the computer. Their company, Microsoft, now makes software, tablets, and the Xbox.**

- In 1976, Steve Wozniak and Steve Jobs wanted to create a user-friendly personal computer. Working in Steve Jobs's family garage, they launched the company Apple and debuted the Apple 1 desktop.

Apple 1 desktop

CULTURE AND EVENTS OF THE 1970S AND 1980S

- From 1964 to 1975, America was embroiled in the Vietnam War. Men were drafted and sent overseas, while antiwar protests and opposition divided Americans. Three million people died, including 58,000 Americans.

★ **In 1972, Richard Nixon was elected president for a second term. He would later become the first and only president to resign, after covering up illegal activities in a scandal called Watergate.**

CNN debuted as a 24-hour channel in 1980, changing the way Americans watched news and redefining how stories were reported.

PEOPLE TO KNOW In 1981, President Ronald Reagan selected **SANDRA DAY O'CONNOR** as the first woman to serve on the Supreme Court.

- Acquired Immune Deficiency Syndrome, known as AIDS, ravaged the LGBTQ+ communities of the 1980s. By 1989, it had killed more than 100,000 people in the United States alone.

AIDS Memorial Quilt, the National Mall, Washington, DC

On January 28, 1986, the space shuttle *Challenger* exploded after liftoff, killing all seven crew members.

CULTURE AND EVENTS OF THE 1990S AND 2000S

STAT FACT NASA launched the Hubble Space Telescope in 1990. The telescope takes photos of stars, planets, and galaxies as it circles the Earth at **17,000** miles (over 27,000 kilometers) per hour.

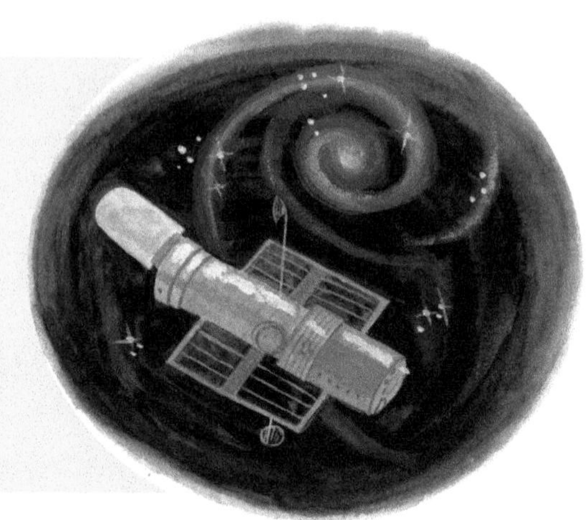

In 1991, British engineer Tim Berners-Lee announced the creation of the World Wide Web, or the Internet.

President Bill Clinton chose Madeleine Albright to be secretary of state in 1996. She was the first woman to hold the position and worked to strengthen America's relationships abroad.

STAT FACT Hurricane Katrina was a destructive storm off the Gulf Coast in 2005. Winds reached **120** miles (193 kilometers) per hour. Hundreds of thousands had to be evacuated, and **NEARLY 2,000** people died.

★ **In 1997, *The Simpsons* became the longest-running prime-time animated television show in the United States when its 167th episode aired. By the end of 2021, there will have been more than 700 episodes.**

➧ On September 11, 2001, a total of 2,977 people died when terrorists linked to the group Al-Qaeda hijacked and crashed four airplanes. These attacks against the United States are referred to as 9/11.

CULTURE AND EVENTS OF THE 2010s TO THE PRESENT

PEOPLE TO KNOW **BARACK OBAMA** was elected the 44th president of the United States in 2008. He was the first Black president and was reelected in 2012.

- In the 2016 presidential election, real-estate investor and TV star Donald Trump beat the first female candidate for president, Hillary Clinton. Trump served one term before Joseph Biden beat him in 2020.

- The *Perseverance* rover landed on the red planet February 18, 2021. The most technologically advanced NASA rover, *Perseverance* was sent to study the Martian surface and atmosphere.

- COVID-19, also called coronavirus, is a highly contagious virus that quickly spread around the globe beginning in 2019. It was mitigated by masks, social distancing, hand-washing, and the development of a vaccine.

- In 2013, Black Lives Matter started as a social media campaign against racism. Reacting to unchecked police violence against Black people, the campaign grew into a national protest movement.

PEOPLE TO KNOW **RUTH BADER GINSBURG** died on September 18, 2020. She was long an advocate for women's rights before being appointed to the Supreme Court in 1993. She led the legal fight against gender discrimination in six landmark cases.

RESOURCES

In 2021, President Joseph R. Biden appointed Deb Haaland to head the Department of the Interior, making her the first Indigenous American to serve as a cabinet secretary. Her history, and other unique American stories, can be found by visiting museums, national parks, online, and your local library.

PLACES TO VISIT

Plan to visit a historic site and/or national park: NPS.gov/findapark/index.htm

Historic sites for history buffs: TheActiveTimes.com/travel/american-history-travel-destinations

Museums to visit: TheCultureTrip.com/north-america/usa/articles/the-10-ultimate-history-museums-in-the-usa

BOOKS TO READ

100 African-Americans Who Shaped American History by Chrisanne Beckner

American History by David C. King

The American Journey by Joyce Appleby

American Trailblazers by Lisa Trusiani

She Persisted by Chelsea Clinton and Alexandra Boiger

Timelines from Black History by Mireille Harper

A Young People's History of the United States by Rebecca Stefoff

REFERENCES

American Battlefield Trust. "Women in the American Revolution." Updated March 25, 2021. Battlefields.org/learn/articles/women-american-revolution.

Andrews, Evan. "9 Things You May Not Know about the Oregon Trail." History.com. Updated October 28, 2018. History.com/news/9-things-you-may-not-know-about-the-oregon-trail.

Andrews, Evan. "10 Little-Known Facts about the Lewis and Clark Expedition." History.com. Updated September 3, 2018. History.com/news/10-little-known-facts-about-the-lewis-and-clark-expedition.

Ducksters. "Renaissance for Kids." Accessed March 25, 2021. Ducksters.com/history/renaissance.php.

Editors of the Encyclopaedia Britannica. "Sugar Act." Encyclopædia Britannica. Accessed March 25, 2021. Britannica.com/event/sugar-act.

George Washington's Mount Vernon. "Ten Facts About Washington's Presidency." Accessed March 12, 2021. MountVernon.org/george-washington/the-first-president/ten-facts-about-washingtons-presidency.

Hansen, Terri. "How the Iroquois Great Law of Peace Shaped U.S. Democracy." Public Broadcasting Service. Updated December 13, 2018. PBS.org/native-america/blogs/native-voices/how-the-iroquois-great-law-of-peace-shaped-us-democracy.

History.com editors. "U.S. Immigration Before 1965." Updated April 20, 2021. History.com/topics/immigration/u-s-immigration-before-1965.

KidsKonnect. "New England Colonies Facts & Worksheets." Accessed March 25, 2021. KidsKonnect.com/history/new-england-colonies.

Mintz, Steven. "Historical Context: Facts about the Slave Trade and Slavery." Gilder Lehrman Institute of American History. Accessed March 25, 2021. GilderLehrman.org/history-resources/teaching-resource/historical-context-facts-about-slave-trade-and-slavery.

National Geographic Kids. "World War 1 Facts for Kids." Accessed March 2, 2021. NatGeoKids.com/au/discover/history/general-history/first-world-war.

National Humanities Center. "Failed Colonies." Primary Resources in US History and Literature. Accessed March 25, 2021. NationalHumanitiesCenter.org/pds/amerbegin/exploration/text6/text6read.htm.

Official U.S. Constitution Website. "George Washington's Farewell Address 1796." Accessed March 11, 2021. ConstitutionFacts.com/us-founding-fathers/george-washingtons-farewell-address.

Román, Iván. "6 Black Heroes of the Civil War." History.com. Updated January 6, 2021. History.com/news/black-heroes-us-civil-war-tubman-douglass-augusta-smalls-galloway.

State of Alaska. "Alaska Natives." Alaska Kids' Corner. Accessed March 5, 2021. Alaska.gov/kids/learn/nativeculture.htm.

Supreme Court of the United States. "About the Supreme Court." Accessed March 11, 2021. SupremeCourt.gov/about/about.aspx.

US Capitol Visitor Center. "Two Bodies, One Branch." Accessed March 10, 2021. VisitTheCapitol.gov/about-congress/two-bodies-one-branch.

ABOUT THE AUTHOR

New York Times bestselling author **STACIA DEUTSCH** has written more than 300 children's books. She started her career with the award-winning chapter book series *Blast to the Past*. Now her résumé includes biographies of Amelia Earhart and Jim Henson, in addition to movie tie-in novels for blockbuster films like *Boss Baby 2*, *Batman*, and *The Smurfs*. Her books include the popular *Girls Who Code: The Friendship Code* and six original titles for *Spirit: Riding Free*. Visit her at StaciaDeutsch.com, and find her on Facebook @staciadeutsch and on Instagram @staciadeutsch_writes.

ABOUT THE ILLUSTRATOR

Barcelona-based artist **IRATXE LOPEZ DE MUNAIN** wrote and illustrated her own children's book in 2010 and has gone on to work for major publishing houses and creative agencies around the world.